SUPERNATURAL
PRINCIPALITIES
AND
POWERS

Other books by Lester Sumrall:

Demons: The Answer Book
My Story to His Glory
The Names of God
The Reality of Angels
60 Things God Said About Sex
Where Was God When Pagan Religions Began?
You Can Conquer Grief, Before It Conquers You

SUPERNATURAL
PRINCIPALITIES
AND
POWERS

by

Lester Sumrall

THOMAS NELSON PUBLISHERS
Nashville • Camden • New York

Published in Nashville, Tennessee, by Thomas Nelson, Inc. and distributed in Canada by Lawson Falle, Ltd., Cambridge, Ontario.

Printed in the United States of America.

Scripture quotations in this publication are from the King James Version of the Bible.

Library of Congress Cataloging in Publication Data

Sumrall, Lester Frank, 1913-
  Supernatural principalities and powers.

  1. Occult sciences—Controversial literature.
2. Spiritualism—Controversial literature. 3. Reincarnation—Controversial literature. I. Title.
BF1042.S84 1983   133   83-12146
ISBN 0-8407-5848-0

CONTENTS

INTRODUCTION

Misconceptions about the devil abound. There are those who write off his existence as simple superstition. Others believe he exists but hold bizarre views of who he is and what he can do. He has been painted variously by artists as a grotesque creature with flaming breath, a little imp with cloven feet, and a hideous, fantastic monster with wings and claws.

But Satan is real. He is not a joke or a myth. He is not a little red man with a tail and horns and a trident. Nor is he, as some believe, an impersonal power, a mere negative influence. Rather he is an intelligent, powerful, and evil being, ruler of the world of darkness. He is hard at work in contemporary society.

I wrote this book because I sense a great need to expose the works of Satan all around us. He is striving feverishly in the world, and we can see it in the increase of witchcraft, Satan worship, spiritualism, and interest in the occult. The word *occult* comes from a Latin word that means "hidden, secret." Satan loves to work in secret, hidden from the light. Paul wrote to the Corinthians that when the Lord comes, He "will bring to light the hidden things of darkness" (1 Cor. 4:5). Satan fears that kind of exposure, like the vermin under a rock fear the light; therefore, exposure is often the most effective tool against the occult.

At the same time, I admit that there is a tension between the need to expose the things of darkness, and the danger that putting the works of Satan in the limelight can arouse harmful curiosity. Paul wrote to the Ephesians, "And have no fellowship with the unfruitful works of darkness, but rather reprove them. For it is a shame even to speak of those things which are done of them in secret" (Eph. 5:11–12).

I am convinced that the majority of people have no concept of the shameful things—many too vile to describe—that go on in the world of the occult. It is a dark, devious, dangerous world that lures unsuspecting people into satanic bondage. So while I must discourage investigation simply to satisfy idle curiosity, I encourage concerned believers to become informed about the dangers of the occult. Knowing the truth is the best way to avoid falling for a lie.

THE DANGER OF DECEIT

In Matthew 24 we read that the disciples asked the Lord Jesus "what shall be the sign of thy coming, and of the end of the world?" (v. 3). Revealing the characteristics of the last days, Jesus described a time exactly like the one in which we live. He prefaced it with a warning: "Take heed that no man deceive you. For many shall come in my name, saying, I am Christ; and shall deceive many" (vv. 4–5).

Jesus' warning implies that the personal integrity of those who claim to speak for the Lord cannot automatically be assumed and that evil workers can disguise themselves as good. Jesus wants us to be wary. In the conflict between good and evil, the lines do not always appear to be clearly drawn. Our Lord wants us to ask questions—to "try the spirits whether they are of God: because many false prophets are gone out into the world" (1 John 4:1). That advice has never been more timely than right now.

I believe our generation may be the one to see Christ return. We can correctly interpret the times in which we live only in light of biblical prophecy. One of the characteristics of the last days is an increase in satanic activity. "Evil men and seducers shall wax worse and worse, deceiving, and being deceived," Paul wrote Timothy (2 Tim. 3:13). "But," he admonished the young man, "continue thou in the things which thou hast learned and hast been assured of, knowing of whom thou hast learned them; and that from a child thou hast known the holy scriptures, which are able to make thee wise unto salvation through faith which is in Christ Jesus" (vv. 14–15).

The only way to protect ourselves from being deceived is to be firmly grounded in the truth as God has given it to us in His Word. We need to know all we can from God's perspective—especially about our enemies in the conflict and their tactics.

I am excited to be alive in this age. It is not an easy time, but it is an exciting, challenging, rewarding one. This moment is crucial to the history of the world. God is at work. So is the devil. If we are not fighting on God's side, we are helping Satan's cause. If we are to wage an effective battle against Satan, we need to know the truth. This book is offered to help you gain insight into some of Satan's tactics and how to deal with his evil minions. Are you ready for the challenge we face?

1

WHAT IS THE APPEAL OF THE OCCULT?

We are witnessing a revival of interest in occult-ism in our nation. Witchcraft, astrology, sorcery, Satan worship, and other similar practices are on the rise. Millions of young people are playing games with the occult. Motion pictures and television shows reflect the popularity of occult themes; demon possession and satanism have become common subjects of the entertainment media. Palm readers, mediums, and witches are perhaps more visible now than they have been at any time in our history.

Satan loves it. He is the one who controls the demonic power behind every kind of occult activity. God expressly forbids any kind of involvement in the occult. He commanded the Israelites:

There shall not be found among you any one that maketh his son or his daughter to pass through the fire, or that useth divination, or an observer of times, or an enchanter, or a witch, or a charmer, or a consulter with familiar spirits, or a wizard, or a necromancer. For all that do these things are an abomination unto the LORD: and because of these abominations the LORD thy God doth drive them out from before thee (Deut. 18:10–12).

In other words, occult activity is so offensive to God that because of it, He drove the Canaanites out of the land. According to 1 Chronicles 10:13–14, Saul forfeited the kingdom and died because he consulted a medium. In fact, under the Old Testament law, death was the penalty for occult involvement. Leviticus 20:27 states, "A man also or woman that hath a familiar spirit, or that is a wizard, shall surely be put to death: they shall stone them with stones: their blood shall be upon them."

Nevertheless, the appeal of the occult is strong. Some people are drawn into satanic practices by the promises of prestige and influence. Others are mystified by the strange phenomena and desire to investigate them further. Still others are influenced by friends and relatives to experiment with what may at first appear to be a harmless diversion but turns out to be a satanic practice. Virtually every major newspaper in our nation has a daily astrology column. For many people who would not otherwise dabble in the occult, those columns can be an introduction to the demonic realm.

Satan is subtle. His most vicious traps may at first seem harmless. But Satan's power is unrelenting, and even the slightest occult involvement tends to fuel the desire for more. Before he knows it, the curious experimenter has become an enslaved practitioner.

Look closely at some of the appeals Satan uses to coax people into the world of the occult.

POWER

One lure Satan uses to draw people into involvement with demons is the promise of power. The quest for power was the very thing that led to Satan's fall. His desire to be like God was nothing more than a craving for power and glory. He understands the desire for power, and he uses it effectively to entice people into his realm.

Occult abilities themselves are called "powers." Mind reading, prognostication, levitation, fortune-telling, psychic healing, magic writing, astral projection, and all the forms of witchcraft, voodoo, and magic are but a few of the powers demons can give to those who seek them.

Virtually every major occult activity promises power, from the basest forms of primitive tribal voodoo to the sophisticated brands of witchcraft practiced in Europe and America.

Occult practitioners admit that the single determiner of status in the world of the occult is power. That entire world, from Satan and the demons on down, is consumed by a desire to control others. Consequently, it is a world governed by fear, superstition, curses, and lies; and in that world, power is all that matters.

I have dealt with witch doctors, sorcerers, witches, and other people entangled in occultism, and I am amazed at what they will do in their pursuit of power. Many have cut off fingers, toes, or ears as offerings to the evil spirits that control them. Others tell me they have fasted and prayed regularly to receive demon power.

Arlindo Barbosa de Olivera, a former witch doctor from Brazil, who also used to work in the office of the Brazilian president, told me that he used to drink hot chicken blood to appease the demons that controlled him. He also would cut himself and mix his own blood with wine as an offering to the evil spirits. Arlindo was converted to Christ and renounced his occult powers to serve the Lord. He has spoken with me in evangelistic meetings across the country.

Arlindo was a powerful witch doctor, head of the *Congere*, a sect forbidden by law in Rio de Janiero. He had the ability to speak in foreign languages he had not studied, predict international political events, heal, and place people under enchantments. He is convinced that all those powers were demonic, and he says they ruined his life. Before he met Christ, despite all the power he had, he was miserable.

In the Western world, we are not often exposed to the intense forms of demonic power widely sought by people in many under-developed countries. I have met demon-controlled people who could walk barefoot on white-hot coals, eat glass, pierce their skin without bleeding, levitate, and perform other amazing supernatural feats. They do it to demonstrate their power.

Whether we see it or not, however, that kind of demonic power is prevalent in our country as well. Satan worshipers and witches practice black magic and sorcery in almost every major city, and they claim to have astounding super-natural powers.

Simon, a sorcerer who professed conversion to Christ, never renounced the quest for super-natural power that had drawn him into the occult. He saw the apostles lay hands on some people of Samaria who had believed in Christ, and the Samaritans received the Holy Spirit. Simon wanted that power for himself.

And when Simon saw that through laying on of the apostles' hands the Holy Ghost was given, he offered them money, saying, Give me also this power, that on whomsoever I lay hands, he may receive the Holy Ghost. But Peter said unto him, Thy money perish with thee, because thou hast thought that the gift of God may be purchased with money. Thou hast neither part nor lot in this matter: for thy heart is not right in the sight of God (Acts 8:18–21).

That account is rich with truth, but its key point is that God's power is not available from occultism; it is not for sale; it is available only through the Holy Spirit; and the main prerequisite is a heart that is right in the sight of God.

This is why the promise of Satan's power is so elusive: he cannot offer unconditional power, and he cannot offer the richest kind of spiritual power—the power of the Holy Spirit. Everlasting power is available only to those who have genuinely trusted Christ and have allowed Him to make their hearts pure.

KNOWLEDGE

Another ploy Satan uses to entice people into occult involvement is the promise of knowledge. The most ferocious spiritual battles are usually the ones that take place in the mind, and Satan's most deadly weapons are those directed at the human intellect. Lust, greed, hatred, and perverse desires all begin in the mind. But one of Satan's subtlest and most effective attacks on the human mind is the promise of knowledge.

It is the same lie with which the serpent beguiled Eve: ". . . your eyes shall be opened, and ye shall be as gods, knowing good and evil" (Gen. 3:5). If only they would obey Satan, they could learn things God had hidden from them—or so the serpent said, and so Eve believed.

The lie is still working today. Consider how many occult practices promise knowledge of hidden things: all kinds of fortune-telling, necromancy, and communication with demonic spirits. Spiritualists claim that they can get in touch with your dead relatives, and through them you can learn secrets you have always wanted to know. Crystal-gazers claim to be able to tell you about things you cannot see. Palm readers say they can tell you what course your life will take. They are all false prophets.

That does not keep people from throwing away their money to hear the lies. At the beginning of every year, famous seers and prophetesses make their predictions of what will happen, and nearly every check-out counter in America heralds their prophecies. Despite the fact that they are usually wrong, gullible souls shell out millions of dollars to find out what they have to say.

The promise of knowledge, however, is a lie, like the serpent's promise to Eve. The devil is not capable of telling the truth unmixed with a lie. Jesus said, ". . . there is no truth in [the devil]. When he speaketh a lie, he speaketh of his own: for he is a liar, and the father of it" (John 8:44).

PLEASURE

Often the desire for pleasure makes involvement in the occult attractive. Satan loves to entice people with the promise of a good time.

In recent years, fantasy games have become popular, especially among young people. Some bookstores have entire sections devoted to instructions and paraphernalia related to such games. In these games, the player assumes the identity of a fantasy character and embarks on a quest for power. Usually the game begins innocently, with a search for hidden riches or some other innocuous adventure. In the course of the game, however, he will encounter wizardry, witchcraft, and even demonism. Often he will be required to commit murder, rape, and other atrocities—all make-believe, of course—in his quest for more power.

Many young people have become involved in such games innocently, thinking that the diversion would be fun, intellectually stimulating, and exciting. They do it for pleasure. They don't know it is an introduction to the demonic realm, disguised as a game, and many have become hopelessly entangled in realities they did not anticipate. Several youngsters have committed suicide when the fantasy became too real.

Another pleasure exploited by Satan is sex. Sexual perversion is often a part of occult practice. Pornography, homosexuality, and bestiality have strong ties to the world of the occult. That is because Satan likes to corrupt pure pleasures and use them to place men and women in bondage.

Like his other lies, Satan's promise of pleasure is always unfulfilled. There are momentary pleasures in sin; the Bible acknowledges that. But they can never truly satisfy. They always create a craving for more and more pleasure—which results in more and more demonic bondage.

PEACE

A thinly veiled, yet often repeated, lie of the devil is that he can bring peace to those who become involved with him. People frequently get duped into spiritualism because they suffer from grief over the loss of a loved one, and they succumb to the lie that they can communicate with the dead through seances.

Witches and sorcerers sell amulets, talismans, and other good-luck charms with the promise that they will result in peace and prosperity for those who carry them.

Again, though, it is all a lie. I have never seen or known of an individual active in occultism who truly knew peace. The occult world is filled with tragedy, bloodshed, and disaster.

All of the devil's promises are empty. He cannot give satisfying power, knowledge, pleasure, or peace. Those things are available only through the Holy Spirit to those who know and love the Lord Jesus. The only fruits of occultism are bondage, sorrow, and unfulfilled desire.

Don't believe the lie and put yourself under Satan's bondage. Christ can give freedom. Jesus said, "Ye shall know the truth, and the truth shall make you free" (John 8:32). May He give us the grace to see clearly His liberating truth.

2

THE TRUTH ABOUT DEMONS

A few years ago, when the movie *The Exorcist* was first released, national news reports stated that people in theaters where the movie was being shown were fainting, vomiting, and generally suffering severe mental and emotional trauma. The movie was about demon possession and its effects, and although it was not based on a scriptural understanding of demonic forces, it was for many people an introduction to the realm of evil spirits.

Shortly after that I began to receive requests for information on demons from network news shows and other curious people who had heard that I had had experience casting out demons. Everyone, it seemed, was preoccupied with the subject.

Demons are among the most enigmatic creatures in all God's revelation. Some people dismiss them as throwbacks to an age when superstition ruled, but believers in the Word of God know that demons are real and that they are active today.

Bible students generally agree that, although the Bible does not specifically say so, demons are fallen angels who followed Satan at the time of his rebellion against God. All our scriptural knowledge of demons supports that view, and there is no other satisfactory explanation for the origin of evil spirit beings. In Matthew 25:41 Jesus speaks of "the devil and his angels." The "angels" of which He spoke are demonic powers.

Demons and demon possession have become popular topics of motion pictures and books, reflecting more superstition than truth. The Word of God gives us the truth we need to know about the nature of demons.

DEMONS ARE REAL

The Bible is clear that demons are very real. The Mosaic law warned the Israelites against involvement with "familiar spirits" (Lev. 20:27), which were demons. The penalty for such involvement was death. Deuteronomy 32:17 implies that all the false gods worshiped by the Canaanites were really demons, and 1 Corinthians 10:20 supports that view: "the things which the Gentiles sacrifice, they sacrifice to devils, and not to God."

The New Testament mentions demons at

least eighty times. It calls them "evil spirits," "unclean spirits," and "principalities and powers." All the Gospels and many of the Epistles specifically mention demons. Jesus dealt frequently with people who were under demonic influence.

Some have suggested that when Jesus attributed certain afflictions and actions to demons, He was simply accommodating Himself to the folklore and superstition of His day. According to that view, what the New Testament describes as demon possession was really mental illness, epilepsy, or other afflictions with medical explanations.

Such a view is not tenable in light of the biblical record. There is nothing to suggest that Jesus did not believe in the reality of demons. He spoke to them and rebuked them. He commanded them, and they obeyed Him (see Mark 1:27). The behavior of the demon-possessed He encountered cannot simply be dismissed as epilepsy and mental disorder. The demons in Mark 5, for example, were able to speak through the man they possessed, and they had enough power to break iron fetters. No medical cause can explain those phenomena.

DEMONS ARE INTELLIGENT BEINGS

Demons, then, can speak and think and act volitionally; they are intelligent creatures, as an incident in Acts 19 demonstrates. Some men who made their living as exorcists, but who were not truly believers, found that the apostles had power to cast out demons simply by commanding them to depart in the name of Jesus. They decided to try that method, and commanded a demon, "We adjure you by Jesus whom Paul preacheth" (v. 13). The demon's response was, "Jesus I know, and Paul I know; but who are ye?" (v. 15) upon which the demon jumped on the would-be exorcists and beat them up.

From that we can infer that demons have intelligence that surpasses human knowledge. The demon knew Jesus, and amazingly, he knew about Paul. Perhaps even more astounding than that is the fact that he knew the spiritual condition of the false exorcists. The demon could see that although they used the name of Jesus, they did not believe in Him, so he attacked them.

As angels, albeit fallen ones, demons have access to vast amounts of knowledge. It is likely that they even have some knowledge about the future. That explains why the most common kinds of demonic involvement have to do with fortune-telling, astrology, card reading, palm reading, and other forms of false prophecy.

Demons know the truth of the Scriptures, and they even tremble with fear because of it. James wrote, "Thou believest that there is one God; thou doest well: the devils also believe, and tremble" (James 2:19). One of their specialties is corrupting doctrine. Thus, the possession of only partial truth can be deadly; demons like to mix truth with lies to create perverse doctrines. Accordingly, most of the cults are based on great truths married to subtle lies. Paul spoke of such false doctrine as "doctrines of devils" (1 Tim. 4:1).

DEMONS ARE SPIRIT BEINGS

Demons belong to the spiritual realm. They were created as angels, to be "ministering spirits, sent forth to minister for them who shall be heirs of salvation" (Heb. 1:14). Sin has so totally corrupted their reason for being that now their activity is exactly the opposite; instead of ministering to the people of God, they oppose them and the work of righteousness in every way.

Demons cannot be seen, for they do not have bodies. Jesus said, "a spirit hath not flesh and bones" (Luke 24:39). Paul wrote to the Ephesians, "We wrestle not against flesh and blood, but against principalities, against powers, against the rulers of the darkness of this world, against spiritual wickedness in high places" (Eph. 6:12).

Although demons do not possess bodies of their own, they have the power to perpetrate their evil upon human bodies, and even indwell and control them. The New Testament describes many cases of demon possession. From them we learn that demons can speak through a person, control his body, and use it for their evil purposes. In fact, demons seem to have a need to indwell living organisms in order to carry out their wicked deeds. The legion of demons Jesus cast out of the man in Mark 5 begged to be sent into a herd of swine.

I have dealt with scores of people who were demon-possessed, and I am astounded at how frequently demon possession is closely related to sexual sin. The cases of possession I have observed indicate that one of the reasons demons are so keenly interested in possessing a human body is the desire to use it to commit acts of sexual perversion. The Scripture seems to support that contention. Sexual sin is named with other satanic activity, as in Ephesians 5:3, where fornication is mentioned at the head of the list of "the unfruitful works of darkness" (v. 11).

Demons can cause lunacy (see Matt. 17:15), dumbness (see Matt. 9:32–33), blindness (see Matt. 12:22), and deformity (see Luke 13:11). Demons often cause people to mutilate their own bodies. The demon-possessed boy described in Matthew 17:15 frequently fell into the fire and the water, and the Gadarene man described in Mark 5:2–7, who was possessed by a legion of demons, cut himself with stones. I have witnessed cases of people indwelt by demons who caused their victims to practice similar masochistic behavior.

It is essential, however, to understand that even though demons can attack physically, the battlefield is spiritual, against unseen enemies who must be fought with spiritual armor and spiritual power.

DEMONS DO NOT DIE

As spirit beings, demons do not die. Jesus said that angelic beings neither marry nor are given in marriage. They do not need to repopulate themselves, since their numbers are not diminished by death.

Demons do not die, but they will finally be punished with unending judgment. In fact, hell was made especially for that purpose. Jesus described hell as "everlasting fire, prepared for the devil and his angels" (Matt. 25:41).

The devil and his underlings know their destiny. When Jesus encountered a demon-possessed man in the synagogue, the demon cried, "Let us alone; what have we to do with thee, thou Jesus of Nazareth? art thou come to destroy us?" (Mark 1:24). The legion of demons that had possessed the man in the Gadarene cemetery said, "What have we to do with thee, Jesus, thou Son of God? art thou come hither to torment us before the time?" (Matt. 8:29). Perhaps the knowledge of their impending doom is what makes them tremble (see James 2:19).

DEMONS HAVE A HIERARCHY

Demons operate under a structured system, a hierarchy of evil. Their sheer number and organization make it possible for Satan to carry out his evil program with a vast network of his evil agents—spirit beings that are apparently virtually unlimited by space or time. They can perpetrate their evil works and communicate with Satan, so that, although he is not omnipotent or omniscient, he is not hampered much by a shortage of knowledge about human events and activities, and he does not lack for workers willing to carry out his evil wishes.

Jesus spoke of Satan's hierarchy as a kingdom. When the Pharisees accused Him of casting out demons by the power of Satan, He replied, "If Satan cast out Satan, he is divided against himself; how shall then his kingdom stand?" (Matt. 12:26).

The terms used in Scripture to describe demons confirm that this hierarchy exists. Demons are called "principalities . . . powers . . . rulers of the darkness of this world . . . [agents of] spiritual wickedness in high places" (Eph. 6:12). They are rulers, authorities, governors of an invisible kingdom of evil.

It is interesting that Satan and the demons have a kingdom. The good angels have no kingdom of their own; they are "ministering spirits" (Heb. 1:14). They are servants—submissive to their Leader in the kingdom of God.

The kingdom of Satan is a cruel, wicked perversion and imitation of the kingdom of God. The fruits of Satan's kingdom are evil, never good. The demons are under Satan's control, and they desire to bring men under their control. In that way Satan would seek to realize the fantasy that led to his fall—that of being exalted above God. Yet the satanic kingdom is doomed to failure.

Demons are involved in a carefully planned strategy to destroy any manifestation of the kingdom of God. Being a believer does not alter the fact that Satan and the demons are enemies. They will attack believers and non-believers alike. The difference is that if you have trusted Christ, you have God's promise of a power that overcomes demonic power—the power of the Holy Spirit. ". . . greater is he that is in you, than he that is in the world" (1 John 4:4).

If you are not a believer you have no such power. You are in a dangerous position, because you cannot win over the satanic plot to destroy your life. Jesus alone can deliver you from the power of darkness and translate you into the glorious "kingdom of his dear Son" (Col. 1:13). I urge you to trust Him now.

3

MESSAGES FROM THE OTHER SIDE?

Harry Houdini, the legendary illusionist, was fascinated by spiritualism, the belief that the spirits of the dead can communicate with the living. Houdini spent much of his life going to seances, exposing frauds and charlatans. He claimed that he had never observed any mediumistic phenomena that could not be recreated by nonsupernatural means.

Yet Houdini seemed to be obsessed with the desire to communicate with "the other side." He made a secret pact with his wife that if he died before she, he would attempt to contact her in a seance, and if she died first, she would seek to communicate with him. They agreed between them on a secret message to be given by the dead to the living.

Shortly afterward, Houdini died suddenly when a blow to the abdomen ruptured his appendix. His wife arranged a seance at the appointed time, but the ghoulish experiment failed. A spirit claiming to be that of Harry Houdini appeared but was unable to repeat the secret message.

For several years, at Halloween, seances were held all over the country in an attempt to raise the spirit of Harry Houdini and receive the secret message. No one was ever successful until after Mrs. Houdini, in a drunken stupor, told a friend the message. When a "spirit" repeated the message in the next seance, virtually everyone dismissed it as a fraud.

In recent years, the most well-publicized spiritualist has been Bishop James Pike, a liberal theologian who, distraught over the death of his son, sought to communicate with him through a medium. He was convinced that he contacted the spirit of his son, as well as the spirits of others, including Paul Tillich, a liberal theologian whom Pike revered.

Pike's obsession to communicate with the dead led to deep involvement with spiritualism. The bishop experienced many fantastic spiritualistic manifestations, which he chronicled in his book, *The Other Side*. Ultimately, Pike's involvement in the occult ended with his own tragic death in 1969. In search of insight from the spirits, he went to the Judean wilderness, where he apparently wandered, lost, for days before he died. Millions, moved by the amazing accounts of supernatural power Pike wrote about, were led to involvement in spiritualism, and the practice of necromancy—attempting to communicate with the spirits of the dead—is enjoying its widest acceptance in years.

THE METHODS OF NECROMANCY

Spiritualism often takes the form of a religion. In fact, spiritualist "churches" in many parts of the country have services, during which they sing hymns, say prayers, and even have sermons. Spiritualists may even call themselves Christian and profess to believe the Bible, but their claim is an empty one.

Actually, spiritualism holds beliefs more like Hinduism than Christianity. Their concept of the afterlife is similar to that of reincarnationists. They teach a basic concept of good and evil but ignore the doctrines of sin and redemption and blood atonement. They deny hell and weaken the biblical promise of heaven by teaching that, after death, the soul goes through levels of a sort of limbo in an uncertain existence, trapped between heaven and earth.

Spiritualists may be good, moral people, but they need Christ. Their doctrine takes away the significance of the great biblical doctrines of salvation and resurrection, and those who ascribe to spiritualism are lost—bound to a satanic system that can only lead them further into darkness.

Normally, spiritualism is practiced with the

aid of a medium, a man or woman who acts as a go-between for the living and the dead. The medium may possess psychic or telepathic powers and have the ability through those powers to bring about startling phenomena.

At a spiritualistic seance, the medium leads a group of people, usually assembled around a table, in a chant. He falls into a trance and is taken over by an unseen external force. At that point, the spirit may speak through the medium, often in a voice distinctly different—possibly of a different sex—from that of the medium, or he may cause the medium to write a message in what is known as "automatic writing." The handwriting may be exactly like that of the dead person the spirit claims to be.

The spirit may "materialize" in a vision known as a *phantasm*—a visible image, often floating in the air. Furniture and lamps also may seem to float in midair. Sounds and voices may emanate from inanimate objects.

Obviously, many of those phenomena can be, and often are, faked. The gullibility of those who believe in spiritualism often makes them easy targets for trickery and imposters. But not all the phenomena associated with necromancy can be dismissed as fraudulent. Scientists and observers have testified to manifestations that could not be explained logically. Bishop Pike described some incredible demonstrations of supernatural power witnessed by many, including skeptics, all of whom testified to the accuracy of his account.

Supernatural forces *are* at work in spiritualism. But they are demonic powers, not the spirits of the dead.

THE BIBLE AND NECROMANCY

The Bible leaves no question about God's view of necromancy. Moses' law ranked spiritualism with the grossest forms of idolatry, including human sacrifices:

> When thou art come into the land which the LORD thy God giveth thee, thou shalt not learn to do after the abominations of those nations. There shall not be found among you any one that maketh his son or his daughter to pass through the fire, or that useth divination, or an observer of times, or an enchanter, or a witch, or a charmer, or a consulter with familiar spirits, or a wizard, or a necromancer (Deut. 18:9–11).

The punishment for spiritualism was death.

King Saul's encounter with the medium of Endor as recorded in 1 Samuel 28 is the clearest biblical account of necromancy. Because of the incident, Saul lost his right to the kingdom.

Saul had been backsliding for a long time, and he sensed that the Lord's presence was not with him. In the midst of a war with the

Philistines, he felt he needed guidance. He must have thought that since God was not with him, he might as well seek advice using the devil's method. In disguise, he approached the medium and asked her to call up the departed spirit of Samuel.

A spirit appeared. Whether it really was the spirit of Samuel or not is disputed by students of the Scriptures. If it were really Samuel, it was because God in His sovereignty overruled the medium's demonic power and permitted the manifestation of the real spirit of Samuel. At any rate, God was the source of the message this spirit brought, and it was a message of judgment:

> Wherefore then dost thou ask of me, seeing the LORD is departed from thee, and is become thine enemy? And the LORD hath done to him, as he spake by me: for the LORD hath rent the kingdom out of thine hand, and given it to thy neighbour, even to David: Because thou obeyedst not the voice of the LORD, nor executedst his fierce wrath upon Amalek, therefore hath the LORD done this thing unto thee this day. Moreover the LORD will also deliver Israel with thee into the hand of the Philistines: and to morrow shalt thou and thy sons be with me: the LORD also shall deliver the host of Israel into the hands of the Philistines (1 Sam. 28:16–19).

The passage goes on to tell us that Saul fell on his face, not in repentance, but out of sorrow that he would be judged. The prophecy was fulfilled. Israel was defeated, and Saul was killed. A key passage in 1 Chronicles gives God's perspective of the incident:

> So Saul died for his transgression which he committed against the LORD, even against the word of the LORD, which he kept not, and also for asking counsel of one that had a familiar spirit, to enquire of it; and enquired not of the LORD: therefore he slew him, and turned the kingdom unto David the son of Jesse (1 Chron. 10:13–14).

Saul's offense, we learn from that, was two-fold. First, it was an act of *disobedience:* "transgression . . . against the word of the LORD" (v. 13). And second, it was an act of *faithlessness:* he "enquired not of the LORD" (v. 14).

THE NATURE OF NECROMANCY

All spiritualism is a sin against both the Lord and His Word. Those who seek advice and communication from the spirits of dead persons are guilty of the ultimate offense of rejecting the living God.

Spiritualism submits people to the most direct form of demonic influence, because the person who engages in necromancy must open his spirit directly to demonic power. The medium abdicates control of his mind and body to the power of the demonic spirit, and those who participate are consenting to the same evil spirit. Nothing good has ever come out of such activity.

Necromancy is a platform for Satan. The only communication that really takes place in a seance is communication with demonic spirits. The evil that has been wrought in the lives of those who have experimented with it speaks for itself.

A young woman consulted a medium after the death of her husband. In her bereavement, she felt that if she could communicate with her husband, she might find comfort. When a voice spoke through the medium and told her things previously known only to her and her husband, she was convinced that his spirit had returned to talk to her.

The woman was not even suspicious when the spirit claiming to be her husband urged her to turn over a large amount of money from his estate to the medium. When the spirit urged her to engage in other occult activities, she gladly obeyed. She went to a psychic healer for a back ailment, and he waved a wand over her back, said an incantation, and pronounced her healed. Indeed, she had no more back problem.

Soon, though, she began to suffer from severe depression and unexplainable fear. She would hear voices when she was alone, and she started to experience hallucinations and a terrifying sense of satanic oppression. She would find herself unable to control her thoughts and words, and she began to black out. Nervousness, anxiety, and confusion caused her to seek psychiatric help.

Her doctor had her institutionalized, but her condition grew worse. She began to see visions of monsters and huge insects, and she tried to take her own life three times.

Then a friend asked a godly pastor to visit the woman. The pastor, sensing the presence of demons, rebuked them, and urged the woman to renounce her involvement with spiritualism. She did and immediately was released from her oppression. She saw that the spirits had only impersonated her dead husband to get control of her. Today she lives a victorious life of faith in Jesus Christ.

Christians should never experiment with necromancy, and we owe it to our unsaved friends and relatives who may be involved with it to warn them of the dangers they face. Christ offers the truth instead of a lie; life instead of death; hope instead of despair; the spirit of love instead of fear; and a sound mind instead of confusion. His Spirit, not the spirits of the dead, is our source of wisdom and power and guidance.

4

ARE CURSES FOR REAL?

The ancient practice of pronouncing curses is not dead. In recent years, increasing numbers of counselees have told me they believe they are living under the influence of an evil curse. As proof, they point to illnesses and personal tragedies in their lives and the lives of their family members. Usually they seek advice about how to be freed from their curse, or they want me to try to remove it.

A curse is defined by the dictionary as "an appeal to God or the gods to send evil or injury down upon some person or thing." Those who believe they suffer from curses live lives of terror, seeing divine wrath in every misfortune.

To most Americans, the whole concept of a curse or hex smacks of medieval superstition. In this "enlightened" age, most people do not put much credence in the idea that someone can say the right words and put another person under an evil spell or curse. Yet the practice is not obsolete, even in our sophisticated society. Last year *The Handbook of Supernatural Powers*, a book that gives instructions for spells and potions, sold 328,000 copies. According to a California marketing agency, the book sells at the rate of 20,000 per month and has been a strong seller for years. Clearly, many in our society *do* believe in the reality of curses and spells.

WHAT CAN CURSES DO?

Most of those who come to me seeking deliverance from curses are intelligent, influential, well-educated people who suffer incredible burdens. Consider these typical accounts:

My friend Arlindo Barbosa de Olivera, who is now a minister of the gospel but once was a powerful witch doctor in South America, had the supernatural ability to put people under curses, rendering them incapable of moving, making them ill, or causing some specific calamity to befall them.

A Midwestern family, following a conflict with a neighbor who pronounced a curse on them, said that their house burned to the ground, their automobile was destroyed in an accident, and two unexpected deaths occurred in the family—all in the space of two months. In addition, they testified to a number of minor catastrophes and illnesses, too numerous and too frequent to be dismissed as coincidental. The neighbor proved that he was not physically present at any of the incidents. Although he admitted pronouncing the curse and publicly claimed that the disasters had resulted from it, he could not be held legally responsible and was never charged with any crime in relation to that family's problems.

A young California woman who was cursed by a witch began to have visions of monsters and demons. She was injured in a fall, and while in the hospital, she began to experience unexplainable choking, shortness of breath, and abdominal pain. Doctors felt that her symptoms indicated poisoning, but no poison could be found in her system. She was placed under careful observation, and nothing unusual was detected. She began to have hallucinations and ultimately was committed to a psychiatric hospital, where she died a short time later.

Haitian voodoo practitioners are said to be able to cause disease, injury, mental disorder, and even death to people miles away, through the use of incantations, prayers, curses, and voodoo dolls. Such accounts are common and well documented in third-world countries, where witchcraft, voodoo, and black magic are widely practiced.

Those are samples of the kinds of stories I frequently hear. There are logical explanations for many of the phenomena often attributed to curses, but I am convinced there is also substance to the claim that curses can have profound and disastrous supernatural effects in the life of an individual. Although curses are often exploited by folklore and needless fear, they are more than empty superstition.

THE GREAT CURSE

The first recorded curse was uttered by God Himself, and we still live under its effects. Genesis 3 records it for us. The serpent had tempted Eve, and she and Adam had sinned by eating the fruit of the tree of the knowledge of good and evil. God confronted them when they hid from His presence:

> And the LORD God said unto the woman, What is this that thou hast done? And the woman said, The serpent beguiled me, and I did eat. And the LORD God said unto the serpent, Because thou hast done this, thou art cursed above all cattle, and above every beast of the field; upon thy belly shalt thou go, and dust shalt thou eat all the days of thy life: and I will put enmity between thee and the woman, and between thy seed and her seed; it shall bruise thy head, and thou shalt bruise his heel. Unto the woman he said, I will greatly multiply thy sorrow and thy conception; in sorrow thou shalt bring forth children; and thy desire shall be to thy husband, and he shall rule over thee.

And unto Adam he said, Because thou hast hearkened unto the voice of thy wife, and hast eaten of the tree, of which I commanded thee, saying, Thou shalt not eat of it: cursed is the ground for thy sake; in sorrow shalt thou eat of it all the days of thy life; thorns also and thistles shall it bring forth to thee; and thou shalt eat the herb of the field: in the sweat of thy face shalt thou eat bread, till thou return unto the ground; for out of it wast thou taken: for dust thou art, and unto dust shalt thou return (Gen. 3:14–19).

That passage actually contains a number of curses.

First was a curse on *the serpent*. He was cursed above all other animals, condemned to crawl on his belly in the dust (apparently, serpents originally had legs).

The curse on *Satan* would cause him to face the eternal enmity of the seed of the woman, the virgin-born Lord Jesus. Satan would bruise His heel (a possible reference to the Crucifixion), but Jesus would crush Satan's head. That is exactly what happened when Jesus rose from the dead, declaring His eternal victory over Satan and the powers of darkness.

The woman was cursed as well. She would experience increased sorrow and pain in the process of bearing children, and she would live in subjection to her husband.

The cursed *ground* would no longer bear abundant fruit; thorns and thistles would overrun it, and it would require much work to cultivate. Consequently, man's food would include leafy herbs as well as fruit.

Finally was a curse on *the man*. He was condemned to a life of work and sweat and sorrow, and ultimately death. In death he would return to the dust from whence he came.

Every element of the curse has been literally fulfilled. Paul wrote, "the whole creation groaneth and travaileth in pain together until now" (Rom. 8:22). The curse continues in effect until the day Satan is thrown forever into hell, God's people enter into His eternal kingdom, "and there shall be no more curse" (Rev. 22:3).

OTHER CURSES IN THE BIBLE

The Bible has many more serious statements about curses. When Cain killed Abel, God said,

> Now art thou cursed from the earth, which hath opened her mouth to receive thy brother's blood from thy hand; when thou tillest the ground, it shall not henceforth yield unto thee her strength; a fugitive and a vagabond shalt thou be in the earth (Gen. 4:11–12).

It was fulfilled exactly as God said. Cain became an outcast and a wanderer. His descendants were an evil race that was ultimately wiped out in the great Flood.

Jacob cursed his son Reuben, who was guilty of sexual immorality with Jacob's concubine:

Reuben, thou art my firstborn, my might, and
the beginning of my strength, the excellency of
dignity, and the excellency of power: unstable
as water, thou shalt not excel; because thou
wentest up to thy father's bed; then defiledst
thou it: he went up to my couch (Gen. 49:3–4).

That too was fulfilled—the tribe of Reuben
never really excelled; they played a relatively
minor role in the history of the nation.

BALAAM AND THE CURSE

The Old Testament account of Balaam sheds
a great deal of light on the subject of curses.
Balak, the king of Moab, hired Balaam, a seer,
to pronounce a curse on the Israelites. Balaam,
although he was not a righteous man, knew
something about the God of Israel. God spoke
to him and said, "thou shalt not curse the
people: for they are blessed" (Num. 22:12).

Nevertheless, Balaam agreed to go to Moab,
although he warned Balak that he could speak
only what God said. "How shall I curse, whom
God hath not cursed? or how shall I defy, whom
God hath not defied?" (Num. 23:8). Instead of
cursing the Israelites, he had to bless them.

Balak was furious. "What hast thou done
unto me? I took thee to curse mine enemies,
and, behold, thou hast blessed them altogether" (v. 11). He felt he was not getting his
money's worth!

Yet Balaam could not curse the people of God. He told Balak, "Surely there is no enchantment against Jacob, neither is there any divination against Israel: according to this time it shall be said of Jacob and of Israel, What hath God wrought!" (v. 23).

THE TRUTH ABOUT CURSES

Those Bible accounts give some important insight into the question of curses. First, from the fact that curses frequently and literally are fulfilled, we observe that a curse is not necessarily just an expression of contempt or of an evil wish: it can carry with it the actual evil effects it pronounces on its object. Such was true in the cases of Adam and Cain and Reuben.

Second, and of great significance, a curse cannot be pronounced on the righteous. God confirmed that truth in His covenant with Abraham: "I will bless them that bless thee, and curse him that curseth thee" (Gen. 12:3).

If a curse is seen as a pronouncement of divine wrath, it cannot affect the child of God, for he has this promise: "God hath not appointed us to wrath, but to obtain salvation by our Lord Jesus Christ" (1 Thess. 5:9). Someone who is not a child of God cannot control or direct—or even discern—the wrath of God. In fact, he himself is the object of God's wrath: "he that believeth not the Son shall not see life; but the wrath of God abideth on him" (John 3:36).

If, on the other hand, a curse is pronounced by an occult practitioner, it is demonic in nature. It has nothing to do with the wrath of God, but is the devil's power in action. Such a curse need not be a threat to the Christian, who has the power and authority, in the Person of the Holy Spirit, to rebuke and overcome all satanic power.

The devil uses the threat of curses and evil spells to make people live in paralyzing fear. I have met people who, from the mere threat of a curse, were terrified to go out of their homes. The power of suggestion alone is often enough to make a curse self-fulfilling. Yet God, who promises to protect us from the powers of darkness, does not want His children to be afraid. "For God hath not given us the spirit of fear; but of power, and of love, and of a sound mind" (2 Tim. 1:7).

If you feel you are troubled by an evil curse and you are a believer, you need not be in bondage. ". . . greater is he that is in you, than he that is in the world" (1 John 4:4). God has made available to you all the resources of His power to overcome the power of evil. Resist the devil, and he will flee. Draw near to God, and He will draw near to you (see James 4:7–8). That is His promise.

If you are an unbeliever troubled by the power of an evil curse, you need to surrender to

Christ and trust Him to be your Savior. He alone can free you from the power of darkness and deliver you into the kingdom of light (see Col. 1:13).

5

THE LIE OF REINCARNATION

I once heard the story of Marie, a Central American peasant girl who, at the age of six, began to exhibit an uncanny perception. She had memories of events that had occurred long before her birth. She correctly recounted things that she could not possibly have heard or experienced. She could describe perfectly the ancestors and family histories of others.

Marie said she remembered having lived in the same village many years before as a farmer named Enrique. People of the village confirmed that a man of that description had indeed lived there, almost a century ago.

As Marie grew older, she began to display even more amazing cognitive ability. She said she remembered several previous lives, in places all over the world. She gave names of seven of her previous identities, some male, some female. In one of her earlier lives, she said, she was a German monk named Sebastian. She was able to speak German crudely, although she had never learned it or heard anyone else speak it.

Marie is not alone in her belief that the dead are reincarnated. Millions, perhaps billions, of people believe in reincarnation, the philosophy of successive rebirth. Worldwide, more than 80 percent of all people believe in reincarnation. Hindus, Buddhists, and Confucianists hold it as one of their basic doctrines. Of course, belief in reincarnation is not limited to third-world countries. According to polls, almost half the people in the United States say they believe they will be reborn in another earthly life.

TRANSMIGRATION OF SOULS

The fundamental concept on which reincarnation is based is called *transmigration,* or *metempsychosis.* It is the idea that the soul is eternal, and after death it moves from one body to another. Transmigrationists say we are locked into a cycle of recurring birth and death. Life, they teach, is never-ending, and when we die, it is only to be reborn in another form. Some believe that a human soul will enter another human body. Others believe that humans can be reborn as animals, and vice versa.

The idea that humans may return to life as animals is a source of much suffering and starvation in Hindu lands, where the doctrine of reincarnation is the heart of all belief. There, in the midst of unbelievable hunger and disease, cows are allowed to walk the streets like people, eating what they wish; and rats are allowed to proliferate and roam freely—all because people believe that if they kill pests or butcher cattle for food, they might be harming their ancestors.

Hindus learn their religion from gurus, who have learned it from other gurus. There is no written authoritative teaching in Hinduism; their beliefs are passed by the gurus from generation to generation. Every guru is seen as a godlike being, and he is worshiped throughout his life and after death. His grave becomes a holy site, an ideal place for meditation.

KARMA

The key to the teachings of the gurus is the doctrine of *karma*. Karma is what determines the state of a soul in reincarnation. Your karma is the consequence of your deeds. If your works have been good, then your karma will be good for your next life. Conversely, if your behavior in this life is evil, you will suffer the consequences of bad karma in your next life.

Karma, in effect, is a kind of miserable fatalism. If this life is determined by previous lives, poor and diseased persons are that way because of their deeds in another existence.

Their suffering pays for their evil and improves their karma in the next life. Therefore, it is better not to help them. The streets of Calcutta are a living illustration of the effects of such a philosophy. Every day, the streets are lined with sick and starving beggars. Then every morning, a wagon comes around to collect the bodies of those who have died during the night. Still, life goes on all around, as millions of people, seemingly unmoved, continue in what seems to be a meaningless existence.

Karma is the ultimate dehumanizing philosophy. You dare not exterminate the roaches and lice and bedbugs that sleep with you, for there is a possibility that you knew them in a previous life. Animal life is as significant as human life, and humanity is as insignificant as a flatworm. Pain and pleasure, grief and joy, become the meaningless vestiges of a forgotten existence.

THE FOLLY OF REINCARNATION

It seems incredible that in a civilized society anyone could subscribe to such a belief. Yet many do, and they point to cases like Marie as evidence of the validity of their belief.

Reincarnation is the devil's lie, however, and the demons are busy doing everything they can to perpetuate it. Knowledge like Marie's is common in those who are demon-possessed. Arlindo de Olivera has told me that he was possessed by a demon who claimed to have inhabited a doctor by the name of Rubenstein. He gave Arlindo enough knowledge of the medical profession that Arlindo could correctly diagnose illnesses and prescribe medicine.

Other demons told Arlindo they had come from South Africa, India, and Europe. They could tell him about people whom they had inhabited before Arlindo, and they gave him cognitive powers similar to those of Marie.

Satan has good reasons for wanting to make people think they will be reincarnated. First, *it is a denial of the resurrection of Christ.* If souls perpetually inhabited one body after another, the idea of a bodily resurrection would be absurd. In what body would the dead be resurrected? And why would there be any need of a Resurrection, since the dead don't really die, but just pass from body to body?

In fact, the doctrine of reincarnation is Satan's perversion of the biblical doctrine of resurrection. Satan is a master imitator. Just as the Antichrist is his alternative to and corruption of the Messiah, and just as his demonic hierarchy is an attempt to copy the kingdom of God, so the belief in metempsychosis is the devil's substitute for God's teaching about the Resurrection.

Reincarnation is *a denial of faith.* The essence of karma is works. If you want to improve your karma, you have to be better. You have to work harder, be nicer, do better, and earn your way to a higher level in the next life—or so reincarnationists say.

The Bible says the opposite. "For by grace are ye saved through faith; and that not of yourselves: it is the gift of God: *not of works*, lest any man should boast" (Eph. 2:8–9, italics added).

The great doctrine of justification by faith, the heart and soul of the biblical doctrine of salvation, is devastated by the idea of reincarnation.

The paradox of the works philosophy is that it either needlessly degrades men or foolishly glorifies them. It either holds them responsible for unfortunate circumstances that are not, in fact, the result of sin, or it gives them credit for blessings they did not really deserve.

The disciples asked Jesus about the blind man, "Master, who did sin, this man, or his parents, that he was born blind?" (John 9:2). Reincarnationists would have said that the man sinned; his blindness was retribution for the misdeeds of a previous life. However, Jesus said, "Neither hath this man sinned, nor his parents" (v. 3). He then healed the man in a manifestation of God's grace and glory.

Paul wrote, "If Abraham were justified of works, he hath whereof to glory" (Rom. 4:2). In other words, if Abraham's acceptance with God were based on his own personal righteousness, he would have something to brag about. Some think they do. Those who believe in reincarnation and are blessed with material riches and health think that they deserve it because of their goodness in a previous life.

They are wrong. You can't get acceptance with God by working for it. Salvation is by grace. "And if by grace, then it is no more of works: otherwise grace is no more grace" (Rom. 11:6).

Reincarnation and the belief in karma *deny righteous judgment.* The idea that we pay in this life for deeds done in another is ludicrous, and it denies the truth of Hebrews 9:27: "And as it is appointed unto men once to die, but after this the judgment."

Those who think their karma determines what they get in life see no final judgment. Life goes on in an endless, meaningless cycle of moving from one state of being to another, and the only retribution or reward is another trip around the merry-go-round, this time on a different horse.

The belief in transmigration of souls *denies heaven and hell.* Karma is its own heaven or hell, and the endless cycle of metempsychosis precludes any ultimate rest for the righteous or torment for the wicked. In fact, in reincarnation, you may be rewarded after one life and punished after another.

The clear teaching of the Scripture is as far from that as it can be. Luke 16 records Jesus' account of the rich man and Lazarus after they died:

There was a certain rich man, which was clothed in purple and fine linen, and fared sumptuously every day: and there was a certain beggar named Lazarus, which was laid at his gate, full of sores, and desiring to be fed with the crumbs which fell from the rich man's table: moreover the dogs came and licked his sores. And it came to pass, that the beggar died, and was carried by the angels into Abraham's bosom: the rich man also died, and was buried; And in hell he lift up his eyes, being in torments, and seeth Abraham afar off, and Lazarus in his bosom (Luke 16:19–23).

Reincarnationists would have said that the rich man's karma was good; he had money and an abundance of food, and he lived in a nice house. Lazarus, on the other hand, would be viewed as the victim of bad karma; he had sores, he was sick and hungry, and apparently he could not walk on his own.

God looks not on the outward appearance but on the heart. Lazarus had a heart of faith, and God had imputed righteousness to him. The rich man was evil. Both men died, and they went to different places. They were not reincarnated as other beings.

In fact, Jesus continued the account by telling that the rich man begged for a drop of water to cool his tongue. Abraham explained to him that there was a great gulf fixed so that no one could cross from one realm to the other.

Then the rich man asked that someone be sent to warn his brothers, so that they too would not be sent to hell, but Abraham's answer was "If they hear not Moses and the prophets, neither will they be persuaded, though one rose from the dead" (v. 31).

Such is the foolishness of anyone who rejects God's teaching about heaven and hell in favor of reincarnation or any other lie of the devil. Someone *has* come back from the dead—Jesus Christ Himself, and He was victorious over death and hell. His testimony, as well as the testimony of Moses and the prophets—and the rest of Scripture—is that each man has one chance at life, and each man must die and face the judgment. The only salvation is by faith in Him.

Jesus told Nicodemus, "Except a man be born again, he cannot see the kingdom of God" (John 3:3). He was not talking about the rebirth of reincarnation; he was talking about a spiritual rebirth, "Being born again, *not of corruptible seed*, but of incorruptible, by the word of God, which liveth and abideth for ever" (1 Pet. 1:23, italics added).

Reincarnation is a deadly, debasing lie of the devil. Eternity is at stake. The only chance to be born again is in this life. How you respond to Christ now determines whether you spend eternity with Him or separated from Him.

6

THE CULT OF CABALA

In the first-century church, one of the most pernicious dangers was the error of Gnosticism. Much of the New Testament was written specifically to refute that subtle and dangerous doctrine.

At its heart, the Gnostic teaching was an emphasis on intellectualism (the word *gnosis* is Greek for "knowledge"). Gnosticism claimed to be a level of wisdom attainable only by those who knew the right secrets. It was the original cult. While denying the major doctrines of the Christian faith, such as the deity of Christ, His bodily resurrection, and salvation by faith, Gnosticism nevertheless claimed to be based on the Bible.

Gnosticism is still alive in many forms and under various names. Theosophy, Christian Science, Mormonism—indeed, all the major cults—have elements of the Gnostic heresy.

Their adherents claim to be "enlightened," privy to knowledge most of us do not have. While purporting to teach doctrine based on the Word of God, they in fact distort and confuse the Scriptures and actually are the enemies of truth.

One group that is not well known but is extremely influential is a sect known as Cabala. Cabala is an ancient, esoteric, satanic cult that grew out of a mystical interpretation of the Hebrew Scriptures. It is a secret, exclusive group whose doctrines are handed down orally from one generation to another in order to preserve secrecy and exclusivity. I have chosen to examine it because it epitomizes the worst kinds of doctrines and practice that come out of the kingdom of darkness.

EVERYTHING EMANATED FROM GOD

Cabala sees the universe as coming from God, but not in the sense Christianity historically has believed. Cabalists teach a doctrine known as *sephiroth*, which states that God's attributes are actual beings, emanations from Him. Out of those emanations came everything in the universe.

The doctrine of sephiroth is a complex, elaborate explanation of how the universe in four realms came from God in four levels of ten emanations, divided into higher and lower emanations. If that seems obscure and hard to understand, it is.

Sephiroth is a strange mixture of pantheism and the Judeo-Christian doctrine of transcendence. Its ultimate effect is that it makes God impersonal, uncaring, and far removed from His creation.

HIDDEN MEANINGS IN SCRIPTURE?

Cabala uses complex and incredible methods for seeking hidden meanings in the words of Scripture. Members of this group see deep symbolism in the simplest biblical concepts; they take nothing at face value. Like ancient Gnosticism, Cabala claims that biblical interpretation is only for the enlightened intellectual who understands the symbolism, and some of the symbolism suggested is ridiculous.

For example, Cabala might interpret fire as symbolic of light, and light as symbolic of knowledge, and so they would disregard the clear meaning of verses that deal with fire and light and read into them deeper, hidden, symbolic meanings. A verse forbidding the building of a fire on the Sabbath might be taken to have deep meaning about the pursuit of knowledge.

NOTARIKON

One of Cabala's methods for decoding Scripture is *notarikon*, a system of using the initial letters of words in a sentence to form new words. As a contrived example, this sentence contains a hidden word: "Educational disadvantages inhibit children's intellectual upbringing somewhat." By taking the first letter of each word in reverse order, you can decipher from that sentence the word *suicide*. The Cabalist ignores the obvious meaning of the sentence and emphasizes the hidden one. Thus, through notarikon, the Cabalist can take a simple statement about the importance of education and see in it a command to kill himself.

Conversely, notarikon may take a word and expand it into a phrase. A Cabalist, for example, might see in the word *prayer*, the phrase "*p*ublicly *r*elinquish *a*ll *y*our *e*arthly *r*iches." Thus, a command to pray would become a command to give away all your money. That, of course, is another contrived example, for Cabalists work primarily with Hebrew words and phrases, but it gives you an idea of what sort of verbal gymnastics they use to interpret the Scriptures.

THEMURAH

Another Cabalist method of twisting the Scriptures is *themurah*. Themurah works similarly to a cryptogram, where one letter is substituted for another, making a code that is fairly simple to crack. One common method themurah uses is to divide the alphabet in half and make a sort of mirror image, like this:

A	=	Z
B	=	Y
C	=	X
D	=	W
E	=	V
F	=	U
G	=	T
H	=	S
I	=	R
J	=	Q
K	=	P
L	=	O
M	=	N

By that system, the word *tory* becomes *glib*. The phrase "dvzi z xildm" means "wear a crown." Of course in English, *xildm* is nonsense, but because Hebrew has no vowels, words formed by themurah have a greater likelihood of being real words. Cabalists go through the Scriptures, substituting Hebrew letters, and attaching great significance to any words that may by chance appear.

GEMATRIA

A third Cabalist method of interpretation is *gematria*. The practice of gematria began among Jewish scholars as an attempt to prove the inspiration of the Scriptures, and Cabalists assimilated it into their system and corrupted it by using it as a way to *interpret* the Scriptures.

Gematria substitutes numerical values for each letter of the Hebrew alphabet and seeks significance in the sums and factors of the numbers in sentences, words, and verses of the Scripture. For example, the normal way to assign numerical values to the Hebrew alphabet is like this:

Aleph	=	1	Samech =	60
Beth	=	2	Ayin	=	70
Gimel	=	3	Pe	=	80
Daleth	=	4	Tsaddi	=	90
He	=	5	Koph	=	100
Vau	=	6	Resh	=	200
Zayin	=	7	Shin	=	300
Cheth	=	8	Tau	=	400
Teth	=	9	Koph	=	500
Yod	=	10	Mem	=	600
Kaph	=	20	Nun	=	700
Lamed	=	30	Pe	=	800
Mem	=	40	Tsaddi	=	900
Nun	=	50			

Using a variation of that system, dropping the factors of ten and one hundred in the second and third columns, gematria notes that the Hebrew letters for Jehovah *(YHWH)* add up to 17 (1+5+6+5). Similarly, the word for *good*, *tov* (9+6+2), and the word for *first*, *ryshvn* (2+1+3+6+5) both add up to 17. That, says gematria, is confirmation that Jehovah, the first of all beings, is good.

Originally, gematria sought to discover such

parallels and thereby prove that the way the Scriptures are constructed is beyond the realm of mathematical probability. If enough amazing mathematical patterns were found in the Bible, that would be conclusive evidence that divine intelligence is the source of the Bible. A great amount of such evidence was accumulated, and books on the subject of biblical numerology and gematria have been written by sincere men of God, showing fantastic numerical patterns in the words of Scripture.

Although that may seem to be a harmless application of gematria, it is in fact a potentially deadly system of Bible study, because it looks beyond the clear teaching of Scripture for unnecessary confirmation of the truth. Besides, numbers can be manipulated to prove almost anything.

Cabalist gematria is biblical numerology gone wild. The Cabalist interpreter ignores the clear meaning of Scripture, substituting fanciful, superstitious interpretations based on the wildest conceivable "meanings" he sees in the numbers. He is more interested in the letters of the text than in the words, more concerned with the intellectual exercise than with the truth.

THE ERROR OF CABALA

The basic error of the Cabalist system is that it sees the Word of God as a riddle to be deciphered rather than truth to be obeyed. Notarikon, themurah, and gematria distort the Scriptures rather than explain them, and that has devastating effects on the lives of Cabalists.

Cabala has historically led to occult involvement and demonic influence. The cults of theosophy and Rosicrucianism grew out of Cabala. It has close ties with spiritualism, witchcraft, and other occult practices. The word *occult* itself means "hidden," and perhaps it is Cabala's preoccupation with the hidden and obscure that has given it so many of the characteristics of occultism.

Worst of all, adherents of Cabala are oblivious to the truth. By implying that the Word of God is hard to understand, they take away the incentive to learn what God has to say. By assigning fanciful and superstitious meanings to the words of Scripture, they negate the truth it contains. Cabala is therefore an effective tool for Satan, whose activity is to "[blind] the minds of them that believe not, lest the light of the glorious gospel of Christ . . . should shine unto them" (2 Cor. 4:4). Although it claims to be intellectually enlightening and stimulating, Cabala is a system of darkness and blindness.

It was against a similar system that Paul warned the Colossians, "Beware lest any man spoil you through philosophy and vain deceit, after the tradition of men, after the rudiments of the world, and not after Christ" (Col. 2:8).

God does not want us to try to decipher

cryptic meanings in Scripture; He wants us to obey its clear commandments. Peter wrote to the Jews in exile, "no prophecy of the scripture is of any private interpretation" (2 Pet. 1:20). The word *private* in that verse could be translated *secret*. God has not hidden His truth in cryptograms and word puzzles. He has given it to us in specific, easily understood language, and it is there for the smallest child to understand.

7

FORTUNE-TELLERS: SATAN'S FALSE PROPHETS

Almost everyone is concerned about the future. As world events become more ominous, and problems like runaway inflation, unemployment, world political unrest, hunger, and disease seem to be growing and affecting more people in our world, our interest in future events becomes more and more intense.

Our preoccupation with the future is reflected in the books we read, in the movies we watch, and in the things we talk about. *Future Shock*, by Alvin Toffler, now more than a decade old, is one example. When that book was first released, it met with enthusiastic response. It shot up on the best-seller list and spawned literally hundreds of other books and movies, all concerned with the question of what the future holds. In college libraries across the country, *Future Shock* is still one of the ten most widely read books.

Satan is cashing in on our concern about the future. One of the phenomena that have grown out of our passion to know the future is the revival of many ancient forms of prognostication, known as fortune-telling. Every form of fortune-telling known to man is either demonic or fraudulent; yet fortune-tellers flourish nationwide as unsuspecting people seek out their advice.

PALM READING

Palm readers claim to be able to tell about a person's future by interpreting the lines in his hand. The lines of the palm are assigned significance—the four lines are the heart line, the head line, the life line, and the fate line. The hand is sectioned into seven "mounds," corresponding to the seven planets of astrology. The palm reader supposedly interprets the placement of the lines and mounds and is able to foretell events in the person's life.

Most palm readers, however, are frauds. A parapsychologist researcher allowed more than two hundred palm readers to read his palm, and no two of them agreed on even the remotest point of their predictions.

A Christian college student met a prominent palm reader on a Chicago street. Recognizing her, he confronted her and began to share the gospel with her. In the course of their conversation, she admitted to him that she could not interpret palms but that she got her predictions from unseen spirits that communicated with her.

Clearly, she was a demon-controlled prognosticator. No one can really tell the future from the lines in a person's hand.

CARD LAYING

Card laying, or *cartomancy*, uses a special deck of cards, known as Tarot cards, to predict the future. Each card has a specific meaning, and the card reader constructs his prediction, based on an interpretation of the meanings of the cards in the order they come up.

The subject shuffles the deck and returns it to the card layer, who begins to turn the cards over and lay them on the table in the order in which they come up. Then he interprets their meaning.

Those who have watched card layers say that their predictions rarely bear any obvious relationship to the supposed meanings of the individual cards. Card laying, in reality, works like all other forms of fortune-telling—the prognostications are messages from demonic spirits. Obviously, no random assortment of cards can tell a person's future.

PSYCHOMETRY

Psychometry is a kind of divination that ostensibly relies on the spiritual aura of an object to furnish facts about the individual who owns it or who last touched it. For example, the diviner will hold the clothing of a missing person and get a mental image of the place where the person can be found. Psychics have used psychometry to find lost items, diagnose diseases, and foretell the future.

One of the best-known psychics who uses this method is Peter Hurkos. Famed for his involvement in difficult criminal investigations, Hurkos took part in the probe into the cases of the Boston Strangler and the murders of several coeds in Michigan in the early 1970s. Hurkos took clothing that had belonged to the victims and tried to describe the killer to the police. Though his descriptions were too vague in those cases to be of much value to the police, in a few other investigations he has led police to the bodies of victims and, in at least one case, to the killer.

Psychometry is simply another form of demon-inspired prognostication. The psychic power that makes it work is clearly the work of the powers of darkness, and the Bible forbids it.

THE FALLACY OF FORTUNE-TELLING

Psychics use dozens of other methods to predict the future and see the unknown. Among them are crystal gazing, tea-leaf reading, and use of a rod and pendulum. All the methods of occult prognostication have three things in common: they are frequently wrong; they are contrary to Scripture; and they rely on demonic forces to give them credibility.

It amazes me that people will put their faith in a person or method that in the past has proved fallible. No matter how wrong psychic prophets are—and no matter how often they are wrong—people still spend their money to find out what they have to say. That is the nature of demonic bondage. It totally disregards the facts; it is blinded to reality.

GOD'S ANSWER TO THE PSYCHICS

God's Word is clear on how we are to judge false prophets:

> And if thou say in thine heart, How shall we know the word which the LORD hath not spoken? When a prophet speaketh in the name of the LORD, if the thing follow not, nor come to pass, that is the thing which the LORD hath not spoken, but the prophet hath spoken it presumptuously; thou shalt not be afraid of him (Deut. 18:21–22).

Despite their poor records, false prophets flourish. Satan takes advantage of the natural curiosity of mankind to know the future. Man differs from the animals in that he is capable of contemplating himself and his future. That self-consciousness leads to fear in unregenerate man. He desires to know what will happen, and so he holds on to Satan's lies as if they were his only hope.

The believer, however, has no need to fear the future. Death holds no threat, and God has promised to supply all our needs. The Scriptures tell us all we need to know about future events. We are victorious over fear and confusion as we look to God's Word for guidance and trust Him with the details of the future.

8

ASTROLOGY IN THE AGE OF AQUARIUS: DO THE STARS INFLUENCE OUR LIVES?

Astrology is enjoying an ascendancy unparalleled since the fall of Babylon. The interest in astrology in America borders on obsession— more than a hundred million Americans are devoted to astrology, and another forty million dabble in it. A popular song more than a decade ago proclaimed the dawn of the "the age of Aquarius," and millions took it to heart. Belief in astrology is simply assumed in many circles, and the question "What's your sign?" has become a standard greeting.

WHAT IS ASTROLOGY?

Astrology (not to be confused with *astronomy*, which is the legitimate, scientific study of heavenly bodies) is an ancient practice, a pseudoscientific method of predicting events by charting the placement of the sun, moon, stars, and planets. Astrologers claim to be able to forecast and analyze events by deciphering supernatural meanings in the positions of heavenly bodies. They say that by observing the stars' and planets' proximity to one another at the moment of an individual's birth, they can predict significant events in his life. Astrologers also claim to be able to predict happenings in the world's political, economic, and social realms and to analyze personality traits of people as they are influenced by the stars.

Astrology is not new; it is one of the oldest occult practices known to man. The earliest records of Mesopotamian civilization contain references to astrology. The belief that the stars influence the courses of our lives grew out of the ancient superstition that the stars were gods, suspended in the sky to observe and determine world events. That explains why the planets and constellations all have names from pagan mythology. Early astronomers carefully charted the heavens and devised the elaborate system of the zodiac, which has remained substantially the same in modern astrology.

When astrology originated, the only known planets were Mercury, Venus, Mars, Jupiter, and Saturn. Together with the sun and moon, they were thought to be seven deities that inhabited twelve "houses" in the sky. The houses correspond to the twelve constellations that make up the signs of the zodiac—Aquarius,

Pisces, Aries, Taurus, Gemini, Cancer, Leo, Virgo, Libra, Scorpio, Sagittarius, and Capricorn.

Astrology is big business. Every major newspaper in our country has a daily horoscope. It is estimated that in the United States more than 10,000 people are employed full-time—and at least 175,000 more persons spend at least part of their working day—in the preparation and publication of horoscopes. For the right price, individuals can order detailed personal astrological charts. The American Astrological Association claims to have sold more than half a million such customized charts between 1977 and 1981.

WHAT THE STARS TELL US

All of that, of course, is nonsense, according to the Bible. The stars cannot tell the future; they were never intended to. In no way do they influence the course of human history. God's Word is specific about what we can actually learn from the stars.

At Creation God said:

> Let there be lights in the firmament of the heaven to divide the day from the night; and let them be for signs, and for seasons, and for days, and years: and let them be for lights in the firmament of the heaven to give light upon the earth (Gen. 1:14).

I see in that a threefold purpose for the sun, moon, and stars.

First, *they divide the day from the night.* Before the days of electricity and television the heavenly bodies determined when people went to bed and got up. Good lighting was impossible or impractical, and not much could be done in the dark, so it made sense to go to bed. The day was over when the sun went down. When the sun came up again, the activity of the new day began. That was God's plan. The daytime served the purpose of allowing people to get their work done, and the nighttime brought the opportunity for rest.

The heavenly bodies have a second God-ordained function: *they serve as a calendar.* The phrase "let them be for signs, and for seasons, and for days, and years" means that the stars were designed by God to measure the movement of seasons and years. The word *signs* means "signposts"—the stars are not omens. In many ways the stars are superior to our modern calendars. They can be used to tell direction and time as well as month and season, and they don't have to be adjusted by leap years.

Ancient people were able to design sophisticated methods for using the stars as a calendar. It has been proved, for example, that the ruins of Stonehenge, a circular arrangement of gigantic monoliths on the plains of England, are actually the remains of an elaborate astronomical calendar. The ancient people who constructed it apparently had an incredible amount of knowledge about the movement of the stars and planets. They were able to use the circle of monoliths to measure that movement and predict, among other things, the summer and winter solstice, appearances of comets, and the exact times of solar and lunar eclipses.

Finally, the sun, moon, and stars serve an obvious functional purpose: *they give light to the earth*. Jeremiah 31:35–36 confirms that:

> Thus saith the LORD, which giveth the sun for a light by day, and the ordinances of the moon and of the stars for a light by night. . . . If those ordinances depart from before me, saith the LORD, then the seed of Israel shall cease from being a nation before me for ever.

THE LIGHT OF THE WORLD

That verse implies that the light of the sun, moon, and stars is symbolic as well as functional. The sun and stars, which never dim or burn out, symbolize God's faithfulness to His Word. God's promise to Israel was that they would not cease to be a nation before Him as long as the sun and moon and stars continue to give their light. He has kept that promise to Israel and will do so until the day comes when there will be "no need of the sun, neither of the moon, to shine in it" (Rev. 21:23), and the glory of the Lamb will be the light.

The symbolism in the heavenly bodies goes beyond that. Jesus said, "I am the light of the world: he that followeth me shall not walk in darkness, but shall have the light of life" (John 8:12). The spiritual light radiated by Jesus Christ is pictured in creation by the sun and stars. Just as they exist to give visible light in the darkness and divide the night and day, so He was manifested to be a light in the midst of our night of spiritual darkness.

John wrote, "And the light shineth in darkness; and the darkness comprehended it not" (John 1:5). "Men loved darkness rather than light, because their deeds were evil" (John 3:19). Mankind turned away from the light of the world, and chose darkness instead, because their love for sin was greater than their love for God.

THE WAY OF DARKNESS

Romans 1 describes the descent of mankind into the darkness of sin. It began when men refused to glorify God (v. 21). As a consequence, their hearts were darkened, and they became foolish, rejecting the concept of God altogether (vv. 21, 28). Verse 25 sums up their error: "They exchanged the truth of God for a lie, and worshiped and served created things rather than the Creator" (NIV).

The heavenly bodies are among "the created things" depraved men have worshiped, and astrology is one of the lies they have exchanged for the truth. The whole concept of our lives' being determined by deities in the stars is borne out of the darkness of foolish hearts that reject the God of the Scriptures.

The celestial "gods" upon which astrology is predicated prove that astrology is a form of idolatrous worship. God warned against such worship. Moses commanded the Israelites to remember God's law and worship Him, "lest thou lift up thine eyes unto heaven, and when thou seest the sun, and the moon, and the stars, even all the host of heaven, shouldest be driven to worship them, and serve them" (Deut. 4:19).

DEMONS IN THE STARS?

Scripture reveals that false gods like those of astrology are, in reality, demonic powers. First Corinthians 10:20 says, "the things which the Gentiles sacrifice, they sacrifice to devils [demons], and not to God." The ancient worship of the stars out of which astrology grew was actually demon worship.

Astrology and demonism maintain close ties. It is estimated that three out of five people involved in occult activities began their involvement with astrology.

Stars do not really influence our lives, but demons do. The heavenly bodies cannot predict the future; they are inanimate objects, traveling throughout the galaxy on an established course. As intelligent spirit beings, though, demons do have some knowledge of future events, and they use their supernatural knowledge to give credibility to superstitions like astrology. We can be certain that any accurate prophecy coming out of astrology is either coincidental or demonic.

Most astrological predictions are so generic, however, that they could apply to virtually anyone. Newspaper astrology columns are deceptively ambiguous. They contain advice like "Look for a significant insight into your own psyche," or, "Give a close friend special encouragement today." Virtually anyone can, with little creativity, find fulfillment of that kind of "prophecy" during almost every day of his life.

Such nonspecific counsel may seem trivial and harmless, but when the uninformed reader begins to look for correlations between his daily horoscopic tidbit and his life and finds them, his simple curiosity often turns to occult bondage. He becomes unwilling to do anything without consulting his horoscope, or else he makes bad decisions based on the phony advice.

Do not make the error of thinking that Satan cannot use such innocent, ambiguous suggestions to accomplish great evil. The story is told of a woman who shot and killed her husband because her horoscope for the day said, "Today is a day for new beginnings. You have been struggling a long time with a major conflict. Put it behind you forever."

Similar horror stories could fill a book. Satan is a master at using what seems innocent to enslave the unsuspecting. Who knows how many wrong decisions have been made, how many people have been hurt, how many lives have been destroyed, all because people sought wisdom from the devil's spokesmen?

GOD'S WORD AND ASTROLOGY

The Word of God is clearly opposed to any kind of involvement in astrology. In Deuteronomy 18:10, God warned the Israelites, "There shall not be found among you any one who maketh his son or daughter to pass through the fire, or that useth divination, or *an observer of times*, or an enchanter, or a witch" (italics added).

Death by stoning was the penalty for any kind of star worship:

If there be found among you, within any of thy gates which the LORD thy God giveth thee, man or woman, that hath wrought wickedness in the sight of the LORD thy God, in transgressing his covenant, and hath gone and served other gods, and worshiped them, either the sun, or moon, or any of the host of heaven, which I have not commanded; and it be told thee, and thou hast heard of it, and enquired diligently, and, behold, it be true, and the thing certain, that such abomination is wrought in Israel: then shalt thou bring forth that man or that woman, which have committed that wicked thing, unto thy gates, even that man or that woman, and shalt stone them with stones, till they die (Deut. 17:2–5).

It was a serious offense, for not only did it expose the nation to demonic influence, but it obscured the way of truth as well.

Appropriately, when God was about to judge Israel, He pronounced as impotent the false practice of astrology, which had been at least in part responsible for its folly:

Thou art wearied in the multitude of thy counsels. Let now the astrologers, the stargazers, the monthly prognosticators, stand up, and save thee from these things that shall come upon thee (Is. 47:13).

They couldn't do it. A lie cannot stand in the face of the truth.

Astrology is not a harmless diversion, and it is not a source of truth. It is a lie of the devil. The child of God has no business seeking guidance from astrology. To do so is to forsake God's Word for the advice of demons. We must leave the future with the Lord, trusting that He will direct us, protect us, and supply all our needs. He has promised that much, and that is enough to enable us to face the future without fear.

Besides, a believer has no need for astrological advice. God's Word gives us all the truth we need to know about the future, about how to make important decisions, and about how to approach life on a daily basis. If we walk in the light of His truth, we know that no truth can come out of the kingdom of darkness.

9

ARE THERE REALLY WITCHES AND WARLOCKS TODAY?

A number of years ago, one of the most popular shows on television was "Bewitched." The show departed from the normal concept of witchcraft in several respects, the most notable of which was that the witch, Samantha, instead of being an ugly, aged hag who rode around on a broom, was a lovely, attractive woman who used her powers "for good." The show presented witchcraft as morally neutral, capable of either bad or good effects, depending on how it is used.

The fact that such an idea can thrive on prime-time television and in the movies reflects our society's conviction that witchcraft is only a silly superstition. Almost nobody takes witchcraft seriously these days. We criticize our ancestors for having witch hunts and ridicule them for their preoccupation with unseen evil powers. We go to the opposite extreme and dismiss witchcraft as a joke.

The witches aren't laughing.

Sybil Leek, for example, began a campaign several years ago to educate Americans about witchcraft. Calling herself "the world's best-known witch," she has gone on television and radio talk shows, debunking what she considers to be the greatest myths about witchcraft. Here is a summary of a few of the facts she wants people to know about witchcraft:

- witchcraft is not dead (Leek claims there are eight million witches worldwide)
- witchcraft is serious business to those who practice it
- witches are not always ugly and mean
- witches are usually educated people—doctors, lawyers, teachers, and even ministers
- witchcraft is a religion

As we shall see, almost all of what Sybil Leek has said about witchcraft is true, with one major exception. She presents witchcraft as desirable, an alternative to biblical religion.

What she doesn't tell is that witchcraft is filled with paganism, sexual depravity, fear, hatred, power struggles, and the worst kind of demonic oppression for those who become involved in it.

WHAT IS A WITCH?

A witch is a woman who uses sorcery, incantations, and magic to exercise supernatural control over things in the material world. Warlocks are the male counterparts of witches (although the term *witch* is often used, as I will use it, to apply to males as well).

In medieval times, a witch was thought of as one who had sold his soul to the devil. Modern witches may or may not acknowledge their ties to satanism, but witchcraft and Satan worship are in fact inseparable. Most of the ceremonies of witchcraft are satanic rituals.

Biblically, the terms *witch* and *sorcerer* are interchangeable. The Hebrew term used in the Old Testament is *kashaph*, which carries the idea of incantations, spells, and magic formulas. Similarly, the New Testament word for *witchcraft* is *pharmakia*, from which we get our word *pharmacist*. Witches and sorcerers often used drugs and medicines to mix potions as a part of their sorceries.

The connection between drugs and witchcraft is still there. Many practicing witches get themselves into a drug-induced stupor as a part of their rituals. One former witch who came to Christ told of the common practice of cutting off a finger or toe, usually under the influence of drugs, as a sacrifice to the evil powers, in order to get stronger powers.

THE NATURE OF WITCHCRAFT

Witches operate in groups of thirteen, known as *covens*. A coven normally consists of six witches and six warlocks, led by a high priest or priestess. Their rituals are held in secret and may involve drug use, deviant sex, animal or even human sacrifice, and other hideous practices.

The witches remove their clothes, go through a ritual of ceremonial cleansing, and stand nude (or, as they say, "sky-clad") in a circle around the high priest or priestess. They chant, sing, light candles, and burn incense. The leader reads aloud from occult books; then they dance, drink wine, and engage in group sexual orgies. All ceremonies follow a prescribed pattern. In fact, many of the chants and incantations are centuries old.

The so-called Bible of the witches is *The Book of Shadows*, an ancient handbook on witchcraft that includes many of the rites and sacrificial practices used for centuries by witches.

The similarities of witchcraft's rituals to those of Christian worship are striking. Witches practice a form of baptism, although they baptize with fire and water. The high priest passes his hand slowly through a flame and then through a basin of water. With that hand, he then anoints the head of the inductee and says a prayer in the name of Satan.

Wine is passed around and drunk from a chalice in a mockery of the Communion ceremony. Songs that are sung may include Christian hymns, often with the words changed to make them appropriate to the devilish occasion.

HOW WIDESPREAD IS WITCHCRAFT?

No one is sure how many practicing witches there really are. Sybil Leek's estimate of eight million may be far short. Because witchcraft is practiced in secret and kept hidden, and because there is no single organization that takes in all witches, it is impossible to obtain accurate figures.

Evidence shows, however, that witchcraft is growing rapidly. Occult bookstores cite record sales of handbooks on witchcraft. Witches like Sybil Leek are increasingly visible. Several well-known entertainers and rock musicians have flaunted their ties to witchcraft. Black Sabbath, for example, is a rock group that takes its name directly from a ritual of ancient witchcraft. They and many other rock groups sing songs with words right out of *The Book of Shadows,* and perform satanic rituals onstage in their performances.

Practicing witches may be people from all walks of life. Many of them have full-time jobs in the business and professional world. Some are housewives, mothers, even elementary-school teachers.

Witchcraft has become popular on many of our nation's college campuses. Students meet secretly in covens, often on campus as a part of officially sanctioned college organizations. Students may join at first out of curiosity or the belief that they are playing out an unreal medieval fantasy, but they learn quickly that witchcraft is serious business. By then it is usually too late.

SELLING OUT TO THE DEVIL

In ancient witchcraft, an important aspect of becoming a witch was entering into a blood pact with the devil. The witch would cut himself and with his own blood write out a contract with Satan, signing over to him exclusive power over the witch's soul.

That may be downplayed in modern witch-craft (some witches even claim to believe that Satan does not exist), but nevertheless, involvement in witchcraft is a clear violation of God's Word and is therefore a subjugation to the will of Satan.

Satan does not need a contract signed in blood to take control of a person; all he needs is one willing heart. He finds a multitude of them in those who involve themselves in witchcraft.

KILLING COWS AND PEOPLE

Although witches like Sybil Leek try to portray witchcraft as a harmless, even beneficial, religion, it occasionally shows its true colors.

A few years ago, farmers in western Oklahoma began to find cattle from their herds slaughtered in the fields. They knew it was not the work of conventional poachers, for none of the meat was taken—only the blood. The carcass of a cow would be found lying in the middle of the pasture, dismembered perhaps, often beheaded, but mysteriously, with never a trace of blood.

Local newspapers began to publicize the cattle killings, and soon the national media picked up on it. Some speculated that vampires were stalking about, sucking the blood from the cows. Others dismissed it as the work of pranksters.

It turned out to be the work of a coven of witches, who were sacrificing the cows and drinking the blood as a part of their rituals. It was later disclosed that as many as seven covens of witches operated in that immediate area.

Some witches are more sinister. A few years ago, a group of witches sacrificed a young girl in the California desert. They had lured the girl, a runaway, into their group, drugged her, and then cut her heart out while she was still alive. Authorities suspected that the same group had killed before.

A disturbing number of similar cases are on the record. Many unsolved murders bear the signs of the ritual of human sacrifice. All in all, it is not very pretty.

THE BIBLE AND WITCHCRAFT

As a result of some of that kind of publicity, fewer people are viewing witchcraft as a superstitious lark, and many are seeing it as the dangerous satanic influence it is.

The Bible warns of the dangers of witchcraft. Galatians 5:20 lists it as one of the "works of the flesh" (v. 19). Deuteronomy 18:10–12 lists witchcraft and sorcery among the sins for which God judged the Canaanites by driving them out of the land. Under Mosaic law, witches were to be put to death. Exodus 22:18 says, "Thou shalt not suffer a witch to live."

Witchcraft is the worst kind of religion. It honors Satan and puts people in bondage. It is a system of fear and depravity and bloodshed. It is a spiritual wasteland, made up of people who have completely sold out to the devil, yielded their lives to his control. Its only power is evil, demonic power, and its only effect is the destruction of lives.

Demons inhabit witches and rule their lives by oppression. As Christians we need to be warned about the dangers of witchcraft and also to warn others. Don't dabble in such a thing; don't joke about it. If you know someone involved, pray for his deliverance.

The church alone is the antidote for such influences on our society as witchcraft. We must be vigilant, strong, and faithful in warning and beseeching every man. Jesus Christ can free even the most dedicated witch from the bondage of the devil. We must spread the word.

10

BLACK AND WHITE MAGIC

Magic is a fascinating study. Usually when we think of magic, we think of illusionism, sleight of hand, and the kind of trickery that is used by entertainers who saw ladies in half and make birds and rabbits disappear. That kind of magic is not supernatural and normally has nothing to do with demonism or witchcraft.

The Bible speaks of a different kind of magic—magic that transcends the laws of nature and is demonic in character and effect. In the Old Testament confrontation between Moses and the magicians of Egypt, we see an example of the kind of satanic power that can manifest itself in magic.

Exodus 7 and 8 tell us that the Egyptian magicians were able to turn their rods into snakes, turn water into blood, and cause frogs to multiply. All those things were done, apparently, through evil supernatural power.

That kind of magic is an ancient art, still practiced today in many forms throughout the world. Consider these accounts:

A German man is supposedly able to steal milk by magic from farmers in his area. He hangs a towel on a farmer's door, mumbles an incantation, and squeezes fresh milk out of the towel. The following morning, the farmer's cows will not give milk. It happens repeatedly, and the farmers try locking their cows up, hiding them, and posting round-the-clock guards. Yet the man's method is always effective.

A Kansas farmer always had an abundant wheat crop, no matter how unfavorable the weather had been or how poor his neighbors' crops were. He claimed that each year he would say an incantation over the grain and pour a pint of his own blood on it before planting. His neighbors testified that the method never seemed to fail for the man, even in the very leanest years.

A South American witch doctor is able to heal by magic. He specializes in dental work. People come to him with toothaches, and without ever opening their mouth, he treats their teeth. He has them lie on their backs; then he takes a large knife and waves it in circular motions about two feet above their faces. Sometimes the infected tooth falls out by itself, and other times cavities are mysteriously filled.

BLACK AND WHITE

Magic has been used to inflict diseases and to heal them. Some magicians brag that their powers are strong enough to kill, and others claim that they use their magic only for good. Many people make a distinction between "black" magic and "white" magic. It is the same as the "wicked witch/good witch" philosophy—many people think the same supernatural powers that can be used for evil can be used for good.

That is not so. Supernatural power cannot be separated from the beings in which it resides, and the powers of witchcraft and magic are demonic. Although the effects of white magic may not be as clearly evil, the power itself is.

God's Word warns, "Satan himself is transformed into an angel of light" (2 Cor. 11:14). So-called white magic is one example of the way he can make his evil works look good.

WHAT IS WHITE MAGIC?

White magic claims to be pure, and motivated by good spiritual forces. Indeed, much of what white magic seeks to accomplish seems good.

For example, a woman in San Francisco claims to be able to heal through white magic.

She uses charms and incantations similar to those I have seen employed by voodoo practitioners and witch doctors in primitive tribal areas. But she also uses religious catchwords and phrases. She may recite the Lord's Prayer as part of her incantation or end her chant with the words, "in the name of the Father, and the Son, and the Holy Ghost." She employs a crucifix as a wand, waving it over the afflicted part of the body. Many people testify that she has healed them.

Nevertheless, her methods are not biblical, she has no understanding of the most basic biblical doctrines, and she makes no pretense of being a Christian.

White magic can be used to fight the effects of black magic. It is used to remove curses, heal, locate lost objects, and even to deal with marital conflicts.

Care must be taken to distinguish between magical abilities and the gifts of the Holy Spirit. Satan uses white magic to imitate spiritual gifts, and many believers are easily fooled.

It is easy to see the difference, though. The characteristics of spiritual gifts are specific. One who exercises a spiritual gift must evidence biblical faith in the Lord Jesus alone as the way of salvation. A white magician may not even acknowledge that salvation is necessary.

The person who uses a spiritual gift glorifies

Christ. Magicians only call attention to themselves and their supernatural powers.

A spirit-filled person's prayer is intense, meaningful, and according to the will of God. The magician uses the language of prayer only as he would any kind of abracadabra. His is an incantation, a chant, not a prayer to the Person of God.

The Christian with a spiritual gift shows the fruit of the spirit—"love, joy, peace, longsuffering, gentleness, goodness, faith, meekness, temperance" (Gal. 5:22). A magician may use the trappings of religion, such as pictures, statues, Bibles, and crucifixes, but they are mere decorations—magical charms, no more significant than a rabbit's foot.

BLACK MAGIC

Black magic, on the other hand, makes no pretense of being good. It is done by those who openly admit that they are in the service of the devil. Much of the magic of witchcraft is black magic.

The source book of black magic is *The Sixth and Seventh Books of Moses*, a single volume, purported to be written by Moses. It is an ancient book, and its true origin is unclear. Virtually every occult bookstore sells modern editions of the book.

Incredibly, *The Sixth and Seventh Books of*

Moses claims that Moses was a servant of the devil, and that that was where he got his power. It is filled with many similar blasphemous lies, and it outlines in detail instructions for anyone who wishes to establish a personal relationship with the devil. It promises astounding magical powers to those who follow its instructions.

In the front of the book is this promise (really a curse): "To whatever person possesses this book at any time, Lucifer makes promise to carry out his commands, but only as long as he possesses this book."

The book is absolutely clear in its purpose and effect: it is an avenue to satanic oppression and domination, and those who follow it—even those who simply possess it—will find themselves tormented by evil spirits.

The Sixth and Seventh Books of Moses contains spells, formulas, incantations, and instructions for practicing all the forms of black magic. Its methods are virtually identical to those used by voodoo, sorcery, and every other form of occult magic.

Those who use black magic insist that it works, and widely documented case histories indicate it does. Black magicians are said to be able to affect people from great distances, inflicting them with diseases, psychological problems, and other sinister effects.

One black magician had a widespread reputation for being able to cause animals to die simply by forming an image of the animal out of clay, saying a chant over it, and then crushing it under his foot. He entertained at parties by asking people to give names of troublesome pets in their neighborhoods. He would then demonstrate his technique, and invariably, within a few days, the targeted animals would die. Police investigated the man but found that he could not be placed at the scenes of any of the animal deaths, and so he could not be charged.

Amazingly, regardless of the geographical area or social sophistication of its inhabitants, black magic is the same worldwide. The black magic used by Satan worshipers in San Francisco is identical to that practiced by witches in England and that done by primitive witch doctors in Brazil.

In places like New Guinea and Haiti, voodoo witch doctors are widely feared for their ability to cast death spells on people by black magic. It is the same magic used by that man who kills animals as a party joke.

In fact, magic has not changed since the earliest days of recorded history. Archaeology shows that the ancient sorcerers of Babylon used the same spells and charms used by modern occult practitioners.

GOD HATES MAGIC

The sorcery taking place in Babylon was one of the reasons God judged those people. Isaiah recorded God's prophecy: "But these two things shall come to thee in a moment in one day, the loss of children, and widowhood: they shall come upon thee in their perfection *for the multitude of thy sorceries, and for the great abundance of thine enchantments*" (Is. 47:9, italics added).

Scripture is unequivocal in its denouncement of magic and magicians. God's clear word to the Israelites was "Regard not them that have familiar spirits, neither seek after wizards, to be defiled by them: I am the LORD your God" (Lev. 19:31). That verse hints at the underlying sin in wizardry and magic: it is a denial of the lordship of Jehovah God.

The person who turns to magic in search of a miracle is spurning God, the source of all true and beneficial miracles. He is saying that he does not care to be rightly related to God and does not want to seek His help or accept His will. He is turning away from God, the only truly beneficial source of supernatural help, and toward Satan, the only other source of supernatural power.

Furthermore, the one who turns to magic subjects himself to the one who uses it to blind the minds of unbelievers—Satan. The Word of God equates all magic with worship of the devil, and there is no other way to see it.

WHAT'S WRONG WITH WHITE MAGIC?

Scripture makes no distinction between black and white magic. One form of sorcery is as evil as the other, and God forbade both.

In fact, a case could be made that white magic is potentially more dangerous than black magic. By masquerading as something good and thus luring people into occult involvement, white magic becomes a deadly, destructive, enslaving force. Although its immediate effects may seem beneficial, its long-range effects are hellish, terrifying enslavement to the devil, whose works—including all forms of magic—Jesus Christ was manifested to destroy.

11

HAUNTED HOUSES: THE DWELLING PLACES OF DEMONS

I was once a guest in an ancient castle in Switzerland. My bedroom was upstairs in a turret, and I had to take a lighted lamp with me to see the way (there were no electric lights either on the stairs or in the bedroom). The doors screeched—I think every hinge in that house was rusty—the stairs creaked, and the windows were long and narrow. The pictures on the wall all had a dark and gloomy tone.

My hostess was an elderly woman, a committed Christian in her seventies or eighties, and she spent the evening telling me the story of her family. I suppose it was a typical account (if the history of a family who lived in a castle can be called typical), but in the darkness of that castle, the stories—mostly tragic, depressing stories of people who had lived there and were now all dead—somehow had a spooky sound to them.

The only source of heat was a large fireplace, and as the flames from the fire cast flickering shadows all over the wall, I did not feel comfortable about the long climb from there to my bedroom in the tower.

In retrospect it seems funny, but that night I was not laughing. I prayed and rebuked the powers of darkness that were causing my fear, and I was able to sleep through the night without incident.

Most people never spend the night in an ancient castle turret, but all of us know the spirit of fear that can make such experiences frightening. We seem to have an inbred uneasiness about big, dark houses that may be "haunted." We have all heard stories about haunted houses, where spirits seem to dwell and cause noises, strange images, and even physical phenomena. What is the truth about such places?

THE PHENOMENA OF A HAUNTED HOUSE

Ghostlike appearances and phenomena are simply manifestations of demonic beings. Biblically, there is no other way to view the phenomena of a haunted house. We know that the spirits of dead people do not become "ghosts," inhabiting houses, buildings, or graveyards. Any spirits that masquerade as ghosts, then, are demonic spirits. And they may show themselves in many forms, through many means, to any one of the human senses.

Sound is one means by which a demon may make himself known. Haunted houses are characterized by unexplainable noises. Strong rappings; footsteps; pounding; clanging; or soft, rustling noises are typical manifestations, and it is not uncommon to hear human voices. Groans and moans may emanate from the walls, or animal noises or even inanimate sounds, like the ringing of a telephone, may be clearly heard.

Sight is another way through which demonic manifestations may occur. The typical "ghost" is a shadowy apparition, a slowly moving figure or light. Some demons may clearly manifest themselves as persons, animals, or hideous monsters. They may appear and disappear, move through walls, or suddenly change form. Some such "ghosts" appear repeatedly and even regularly. Objects may move around, or be thrown suddenly and violently across the room or onto the floor.

Touch is a sense often associated with ghostly manifestations in haunted houses. The temperature in a room may drop or rise suddenly and unexplainably. The place may have a clammy, sinister atmosphere that seems to cover everything. An evil spirit can sometimes actually cause a physical sensation, such as choking, pinching, or even a hard blow that can knock a person to the ground. Often the demons will leave bruises, bite marks, and cuts on their victims.

Smell is a sense often affected by demonic manifestations. Some demon-infested places reek with a sickening, musty smell.

FAMOUS HAUNTED HOUSES

A few years ago, the book, and later the movie *The Amityville Horror* became popular. The story was reportedly based on the true experiences of a family who had purchased a home on Long Island, only to discover that their dream house was a nightmare. The movie showed red liquid flowing from the keyholes. Green slime oozed from the walls. Overpowering odors permeated the place at odd times. The temperature would drop or rise as much as fifteen degrees in an instant. The place was haunted.

The family was terrified. They began to hear frightening noises, which they could only liken to the sound of an elephant rolling around. They called priests and exorcists to look at the house, but no one was able to help them. They left their home after having lived there only twenty-eight days.

Perhaps the most notorious haunted house is the Borley Rectory in Essex, England. In the 1930s, parapsychologists and researchers investigated that house for fourteen months and logged more than two thousand ghostly manifestations. At one point, a ghostlike nun appeared and asked for prayers and a Mass to deliver her tormented soul. In another occurrence, a coach appeared, driven by a headless man.

Another haunted rectory in England, the Swanton Novers Rectory, became famous in 1919 when water and oil mysteriously began dripping from the ceiling.

A DEMONIC HOUSE

In Java, Indonesia, a pastor friend and I had the dubious privilege of staying in a house where evil spirits repeatedly manifested themselves. The family was used to it; in fact, the man of the house was demon-possessed, and the whole family knew it.

One day while the man was gone, his wife told us his story. He worshiped demons. She showed us a little cabinet he kept in the house as an altar. In the cabinet was a silver dagger suspended by a thread, and an incense burner. When he worshiped at the altar the demons manifested themselves, speaking through him and causing weird phenomena to occur throughout the house.

The man was an influential businessman in the community, and he maintained the outward appearance of a moral, upright man. Yet he was enslaved in demonic worship. He knew by name seven demons that inhabited him, and he was at their mercy. In return, they gave him various occult and magical powers.

The demons refused to let the man's wife

sleep in the same bed with him at night. They pinched her and pushed her out of bed onto the floor. Furniture in the house would move mysteriously, and strange noises could be heard.

In the middle of the night, we saw and heard for ourselves. We were awakened by a strange apparition. It stood at the foot of the bed and called my fellow pastor by name. We both heard and saw it, and we began to pray in the name of Jesus, commanding the spirit to depart. It left, but we were not comfortable until we left that house.

OPPRESSION BY FEAR

Such an experience is a vivid example of the way Satan tries to oppress people through fear. It is one of his favorite weapons.

Through fear, Satan can paralyze our spiritual lives. Fear takes our focus off God. The fearful person feels threatened, and the threatened person is not trusting God.

Scripture makes clear the results of God's ministry to us: "God hath not given us the spirit of fear; but of power, and of love, and of a sound [disciplined] mind" (2 Tim. 1:7). These three resources—power, love, and a disciplined mind—overcome every threat, every source of fear with which Satan could confront us.

The *power* God gives is sufficient to deal with the threat of evil spirits. God's promise is "Ye are of God, little children, and have overcome them: because greater is he that is in you, than he that is in the world" (1 John 4:4). His power is greater than Satan's. "If God be for us, who can be against us?" (Rom. 8:31).

God's *love* works marvelously to free us from fear. "There is no fear in love; but perfect love casteth out fear: because fear hath torment" (1 John 4:18). *Love* is the opposite of *torment*. When Satan would torment us with fear, God offers His love instead. With the powerful resource of God's love, we never need be burdened with satanic fear.

A *disciplined mind* is crucial to a life of victory over fear. Having a disciplined mind means refusing to believe silly superstitions. It means saturating our thoughts with the Word of God. It means having a mind that is given to prayer and to pure thoughts. In such a mind, there is no room for fear.

ARE HAUNTED HOUSES REALLY DANGEROUS?

But are the fears Satan uses against us merely empty fears? Are haunted houses really deadly? What about people who die mysteriously in haunted houses? What should a person do if he lives in a haunted house?

Those are important questions. Satan *is* a deadly, powerful foe, and he will use any means he can to destroy people, as the biblical account of Job demonstrates.

Haunted houses themselves are mere deceptions. The phenomena in them are not caused by ghosts, but by demons. Therefore, a person is vulnerable to demonic forces in a haunted house. The person who walks with God in the fullness of the Holy Spirit cannot be threatened by demons. Yet the unbeliever or the backslidden believer—anyone who has yielded to sin and is out from under the umbrella of God's protection—is in grave spiritual danger from demonic forces no matter where he is. If he is in a haunted house, in the presence of active demonic manifestations, he is especially in danger.

No one should remain anywhere where there are demonic forces at work. If you are in a haunted house, get out. Rebuke the demonic forces and command them in the name of Christ to depart. If you are yourself in Christ and walking in His power, they must obey. Do this in an attitude of prayer, remembering that the power over demonic forces is God's, and you are just His agent. Then in prayer dedicate the structure to the glory of God. That will put an end to the haunting.

12

IS HYPNOSIS DANGEROUS?

In 1958, the American Medical Association for the first time accepted hypnosis as a therapeutic technique. They accompanied their endorsement with a warning that hypnosis can produce detrimental side effects and in many cases is dangerous. Today, though, more than five thousand physicians, dentists, and psychiatrists use hypnosis in their practices.

The recent acceptance of hypnosis by scientists and doctors is amazing in light of the fact that hypnosis is an ancient practice that was always more a part of magic and witchcraft than of science and medicine. Ancient occult practitioners used a form of hypnotism to control people for their evil deeds.

Hypnosis is a kind of mental suggestion, in which the hypnotist lulls his subject into a trancelike state and then, by speaking directly to his subconscious, alters his state of mind.

Hypnosis can be used as a sedative, a behavioral modification device, or even a stimulant.

Hypnosis, for example, can be used to probe the memory. Police have used it to obtain evidence in investigations. Through hypnosis, a witness can be made to relive the crime he witnessed and recall even minute details, such as car license plates, physical descriptions of suspects, and so on.

Dentists use hypnosis to overcome fear, pain, and even strong gag reflexes. Obstetricians sometimes hypnotize mothers prior to delivery to allow them to remain conscious throughout the birth with a minimum of pain. Dietitians use hypnotism to help people control overeating. Posthypnotic suggestion has helped people stop smoking and drinking.

WHAT HAPPENS DURING HYPNOSIS?

Those who have undergone hypnosis describe it as a pleasant, enjoyable experience. The body is immobile, and any response to the hypnotist's suggestions seems involuntary. The mind is in a neutral state of submission to the hypnotist.

That submissive attitude is essential to hypnosis. No one who does not wish to be can be hypnotized. Any sort of resistance on the part of the subject keeps him from entering the hypnotic trance essential to mental suggestion.

The hypnotist speaks in a soft, mild, soothing

voice. When the subject is totally relaxed and open to the hypnotist's power of suggestion, the hypnotist may ask him questions, probe his memory, or command him to do things.

Although many people believe that a person cannot be coerced into behavior that would ordinarily be against his will or moral standards, that fact has not been completely established.

The hypnotist can give a posthypnotic suggestion, which takes effect after the person leaves the hypnotic trance. For example, while the subject is in a hypnotic state, the hypnotist might tell him that he will feel sleepy the next time he hears music. After the subject returns to normal consciousness, perhaps even several hours later, when he hears music, he will immediately sense an unexplainable fatigue.

No one really knows why hypnosis works. Many people are suspicious of its claims, and Christians I talk to tell me they feel that something about it is evil.

Those suspicions may be well founded.

WHAT'S WRONG WITH HYPNOSIS?

Anything that can influence the mind as radically as hypnosis ought to make Christians wary, especially in light of the fact that it is so little understood.

The mental and spiritual openness that makes hypnosis effective is so completely an abdication of self-control that evil powers can take advantage of it. Demons seek a mind that is totally submissive and yielded to their influence, and they may find it in someone who is willing to submit to hypnotism. The ancient connection between magic and hypnotism should not be overlooked. No Christian should abandon control of his mind to any hypnotist.

Some experts believe that hypnosis opens the mind and memory and will to the point that it can be permanently altered by the hypnotist. An effective hypnotist, they say, can erase and re-form the memory like a tape recorder records new sounds on an old tape.

Hypnotism can become habit-forming, like any other sedative or anesthetic. A person who has been hypnotized repeatedly grows to crave the experience like an alcoholic craves liquor. He becomes psychologically dependent on it—sometmes to the point at which he must be taught to hypnotize himself if he is to function.

The claim that a person under hypnosis will not act contrary to his will or moral standards does not mean much in light of the Bible's teaching that "The heart is deceitful above all things, and desperately wicked" (Jer. 17:9). Man has a sinful nature, an inbred depravity that gives him a natural inclination to evil. The Christian who understands that fact knows he is likely to do things under the control of a hypnotist that he would not do under the control of the Holy Spirit.

THE QUESTION OF CONTROL

The real issue in hypnosis is the question of control. Hypnotism is like alcohol or drugs or pornography in that it opens the mind to subliminal influences outside the control of the one affected. That is not to say that every hypnotic experience results in a demonic attack, but I believe it carries that potential, and so ought to be avoided by believers.

Second Corinthians 10:5 tells us that we are to bring every thought into captivity to the obedience of Christ. The person who submits his mind to a hypnotist cannot submit it completely to God.

Our minds are to be stayed on God (see Is. 26:3), and He promises to keep us in perfect peace. The Holy Spirit is to rule both our conscious and subconscious minds. Paul gave the pattern for controlling our minds: "Whatsoever things are true, whatsoever things are honest, whatsoever things are just, whatsoever things are pure, whatsoever things are lovely, whatsoever things are of good report; if there be any virtue, and if there be any praise, think on these things" (Phil. 4:8).

The best way to do that is to saturate your mind with the Word of God. The mind that is transformed and controlled by God's Word has an impenetrable defense against Satan and his attacks.

13

SATAN'S ULTIMATE TRAP

Human beings seem to be easy marks for Satan's trickery. We like to try to draw the lines of definition clearly. We tend to see in black and white, preferring to think that Satan is so utterly and obviously evil that he cannot deceive us. As a result, he has a heyday with us, because we go on blissfully thinking that whatever is good cannot be used by the devil.

God's 'Word corrects that misconception. Second Corinthians 11:14–15 says, "Satan himself is transformed into an angel of light. Therefore it is no great thing if his ministers also be transformed as the ministers of righteousness." That means Satan can use what appears to be good to accomplish his evil plan.

Occultism is not the only way demonic forces can entrap people in the devil's web. In fact, Satan can work just as effectively—often more effectively—in a Bible-believing church than he can in the midst of a coven of witches.

Satan's ultimate snare, the one with which he destroys more lives than with astrology, witch-craft, necromancy, and all the occult activities combined, is worldliness.

Worldliness? Yes, Scripture calls Satan "The god of this world" (2 Cor. 4:4). Jesus referred to him on three occasions as "the prince of this world" (John 12:31; 14:30; 16:11). Paul called him "the prince of the power of the air" (Eph. 2:2). Satan reigns over this world, and worldli-ness—the love of the world—is the subtlest, most damaging, yet commonest form of Satan-ism.

WORLDLINESS IS SATANIC

A common notion is that Satan is the king of hell, in opposition to Christ, the King of heaven. That has the ring of truth to it, but it is utterly false. Satan is God's enemy, not God's rival. His kingdom is not hell, but the world in which we live.

The phrase "the god of this world" is full of meaning. It shows that Satan's kingdom is not limited to the angels that followed him in his sin. His authority certainly includes the de-mons, but it extends beyond them to include this world.

The term for "world" (*kosmos* in the Greek text) means the system under which this world operates. It includes everything temporal and secular—the governments, fashions, culture,

education, philosophies, religions, and moral-
ity of this world. All those things are worldly,
and they may or may not be inherently evil.

THE WORLD IS SATAN'S

Satan's temptation of Christ included the
offer of the kingdoms of the world. Luke 4:5–8
describes the incident:

> And the devil, taking him up into an high
> mountain, shewed unto him all the kingdoms of
> the world in a moment of time. And the devil
> said unto him, All this power will I give thee,
> and the glory of them: for that is delivered unto
> me; and to whomsoever I will I give it. If thou
> wilt worship me, all shall be thine. And Jesus
> answered and said unto him, Get thee behind
> me, Satan: for it is written, Thou shalt worship
> the Lord thy God, and him only shalt thou serve.

It is significant that Jesus' response did not
deny Satan's right to control the possession of
the kingdoms of the world—only his right to
receive worship. Satan's offer was bona fide; he
did indeed control this world's kingdoms, and
he could legitimately offer them to whomever
he wished.

By contrast, Jesus said, "My kingdom is not
of this world" (John 18:36). He said of believers,
"they are not of the world, even as I am not of
the world" (John 17:14). And He told His
followers, "In the world ye shall have tribula-

tion" (John 16:33). The word for "world" in all those verses is *kosmos*, the realm over which Satan has control.

The world is a realm of darkness. Jesus said, "I am come a light into the world" (John 12:46). He prayed to the Father, "The world hath not known thee" (John 17:25). Peter wrote about "the corruption that is in the world" (2 Pet. 1:4), and "the pollutions of the world" (2 Pet. 2:20). Satan uses the world system to advance his evil purposes, and 2 Corinthians 4:4, the verse that calls him "the god of this world," says that he has "blinded the minds of them which believe not, lest the light of the glorious gospel of Christ, . . . should shine unto them."

That is why John wrote,

> Love not the world, neither the things that are in the world. If any man love the world, the love of the Father is not in him. For all that is in the world, the lust of the flesh, and the lust of the eyes, and the pride of life, is not of the Father, but is of the world (1 John 2:15–16).

Near the conclusion of the Epistle, John added, "We know that we are of God, and the whole world lieth in wickedness" (5:19). The word translated "wickedness" is better translated "the wicked one." It is an affirmation that Satan himself controls the world system.

HOW SATAN GOT HIS KINGDOM

How did Satan gain control of the world? Before his fall, Satan was endowed with a position of supreme authority in God's creation. Some commentators believe his realm of authority included our world.

When God created Adam and Eve, it was with the intention that man would "replenish the earth, and subdue it: and have dominion over the fish of the sea, and over the fowl of the air, and over every living thing that moveth upon the earth" (Gen. 1:28). God made man to rule the world.

Satan was jealous of man's position and desired it for himself. Perhaps that was his primary motivation in tempting the woman. The story is familiar. He disguised himself as a serpent and appeared to her in the Garden. And he used all the tools available to him—the lust of the flesh, the lust of the eyes, and the pride of life—to tempt Eve to sin.

Those three elements of the world system motivated Eve's response:

> When the woman saw that the tree was *good for food* [lust of the flesh], and that it was *pleasant to the eyes* [lust of the eyes], and a tree *to be desired to make one wise* [pride of life], she took of the fruit thereof, and did eat, and gave also unto her

husband with her: and he did eat (Gen. 3:6, italics added).

Satan's words to Eve bear a striking resemblance to his own words when he sinned. Remember that he wanted to "be like the most High" (Is. 14:14). He told Eve, "God doth know that in the day ye eat thereof, then your eyes shall be opened, and *ye shall be as gods*, knowing good and evil" (Gen. 3:5, italics added). It was a mixture of the truth and a lie. Their eyes were opened so that they could see good and evil, but that did not make them like God; it made them more like the devil.

By obeying Satan and disobeying God, Adam and Eve abdicated their position of dominion over the world to Satan. Their choice to eat the forbidden fruit was a deliberate subjection of their wills to Satan's. That is how he gained control over the world. From that day to this He has been in control of the *kosmos*.

Apparently, Satan has retained much of the power and authority that were his before his fall. Jude 9 tells of an incident when Michael the archangel disputed with Satan over the body of Moses. Michael did not rail on him flippantly, but rather he said, "The Lord rebuke thee." Even the archangel was careful to acknowledge the inherent authority in this glorious, albeit fallen, creature.

It is Satan who dictates the policies, philosophies, and objectives of this world. That is why

James wrote, "Know ye not that the friendship of the world is enmity with God? whosoever therefore will be a friend of the world is the enemy of God" (James 4:4).

THE WORLD IS TOTALLY EVIL

Everything about the *kosmos* works for evil, although many good things are incorporated in it. Worldly things such as secular art and music are not intrinsically evil; government per se is not wicked; and neither are many of the morals and ideals of the world system. But as integral parts of Satan's kingdom and of this world's system, they are bound by a common evil principle, that of independence from God, and together they work for that single diabolical purpose.

Satan's vast kingdom includes not only all that is in the world, but also the realm of evil spirits as well, what Paul called "spiritual wickedness in high places" (Eph. 6:12). Their particular sphere of influence is this world, where they seek to intervene in the affairs of men to further the cause of their rebellion against God.

Like Satan himself, his kingdom and this world operate on a totally self-centered philosophy. They reject God's authority, God's Word, and ultimately, God's grace.

In fact, Jesus indicated that a distinguishing characteristic of the world is that it rejected

Him. His message to the disciples on the night He was betrayed contained these words:

> If the world hate you, ye know that it hated me before it hated you. If ye were of the world, the world would love his own: but because ye are not of the world, but I have chosen you out of the world, therefore the world hateth you. Remember the word that I said unto you, The servant is not greater than his lord. If they have persecuted me, they will also persecute you (John 15:18–20).

John reiterated that when he wrote, "Marvel not, my brethren, if the world hate you" (1 John 3:13).

Paul wrote to the Romans, "And be not conformed to this world: but be ye transformed by the renewing of your mind" (Rom. 12:2). For a believer to embrace this world's philosophies and ideals is a tragic error, because the worldly Christian is aligning himself with the system that crucified the Lord Jesus.

TWO OPPOSING KINGDOMS

The choice each individual ultimately has to make is between two contrasting kingdoms— the kingdom of light and the kingdom of darkness; the kingdom of God and the kingdom of Satan; the kingdom of heaven and the kingdom of this world. The first is based on a philosophy of sacrifice and service and submission; the second on the philosophy of selfishness, greed, and pride.

One kingdom offers eternal life; the other offers a place in the lake of fire prepared for Satan and his angels.

One kingdom is eternal, spiritual, and pure; the other is temporal, materialistic, and evil.

God's kingdom is as alive and active on this earth as is Satan's, although it may not be as visible. Yet it is sure to emerge victorious. Remember, Satan is not God's rival. God is in control, and He will judge and destroy the power of Satan. Be sure you are aligned with the right kingdom.

Appendix

THE DEVIL'S DICTIONARY

ALL HALLOWS EVE: Halloween, October 31, the night before All Saints' Day. Halloween is considered by witches and satanists as their highest holiday, and on that night, covens of witches gather for an annual festival. Most of the common traditions of Halloween are directly traceable to occult and demonic practices.

AMULET: a good-luck charm, such as a rabbit's foot or a talisman or a special piece of jewelry worn around the neck. Usually the amulet is inscribed with a curse or a spell, or it is actually a capsule containing a slip of paper upon which is written a contract with the devil.

ANIMISM: the belief that inanimate objects are alive and have souls. I have witnessed Chinese people who worship a rock, and aborigines who pray to the spirit of a tree.

ASTRAL PROJECTION: travel of the spirit outside the body. Occult practitioners seek out-of-the-body experiences, believing that they are the source of peace and power. The soul leaves the body and is able to travel great distances and experience things on a different level of consciousness. The practice has long been popular in pagan lands, but it is becoming more and more common in America.

ASTROLOGY: the practice of telling the future by reading the stars (see Chapter 3). Astrology is clearly forbidden in the Scriptures.

AUGURY: the art of divination by reading signs and omens. The one who is able to read such omens is called an *augur*.

AUTOMATIC WRITING: writing done in a trance, ostensibly containing supernatural and prophetic messages. The pen is held in the hand, but guided by spiritual forces to write, often in handwriting style or language not that of the one who holds the pen.

BEWITCH: to influence by witchcraft; put under a spell.

BLACK MAGIC: a form of witchcraft using incantations and potions to cause disease, place people under spells, and contact spirits (see Chapter 8).

BLACK MASS: a satanic parody of the Roman Catholic Mass. The "clergy" dress in black robes and hoods and lead the worship in honor of Satan. The black mass frequently includes animal sacrifices, and in secret, even human sacrifice.

CARTOMANCY: card reading; the telling of fortunes with Tarot cards.

CEPHALOMANCY: a black magic practice that uses a skull (usually from a donkey or goat) for divination.

CHARM: an ornament believed to contain magical power; often a satanic emblem.

CHIROMANCY: palmistry; fortune-telling by reading the lines on the hand. Chiromancy divides the palm into seven planetary mounds that correspond to the seven astrological deities.

CLAIRVOYANT: one who forecasts events through visions and dreams. Some clairvoyants are able to exercise their abilities at will, and others experience the phenomenon on an irregular basis.

CONJURE: to summon a spirit by incantation. Conjurers claim to have access to spirits of the dead, but the Bible makes it clear that they are in fact communicating with demonic spirits.

COVEN: a group of thirteen witches, usually six male and six female, with a high priest or priestess. Often witches' covens assemble in graveyards for meetings that include incantations, Satan worship, and animal sacrifice.

CRYSTAL GAZER: a seer who reads a crystal ball.

CULT: a religious group, usually based on corruptions of Christian doctrine. Cults' distinguishing characteristics include: (1) The claim that this group is the only way to God; (2) a strong individual leader; (3) extrabiblical writings accepted as authoritative; and (4) a denial of the doctrine of justification by faith alone.

CURSE: an incantation or spell calling for harm or bad luck to an individual or family (see Chapter 4).

DEMON: an evil spirit, subservient to Satan, assumed to be a fallen angel (see Chapter 2). Demons can influence those who yield to their power and even control their bodies and minds. Demons are the source of occult powers.

DIVINATION: telling the future or uncovering hidden information by means of occult methods, including card reading, astrology, magic, chiromancy, cephalomancy, crystal gazing, automatic writing, and augury.

ENCHANTER: a sorcerer; one who can cast a spell or do magic.

ESBAT: a meeting of witches to accomplish an evil act.

EXORCISM: a ritual used to cast out demons and drive them away. Some exorcism is itself satanic ritual and is not truly effective in delivering from evil spirits.

EXTRASENSORY PERCEPTION: ESP; the ability to see the future, read minds, and discern unknown facts without the use of ordinary senses.

FAMILIAR SPIRIT: a spirit embodied in a person. The spirit uses and indwells the host person and usually gives powers of divination in return. The Old Testament expressly forbids seeking advice from persons with familiar spirits.

FETISH: an object that is regarded as sacred and magical. Often the fetish is an idol or some representation of a demonic spirit, but it may be an abstract object as well.

FIRE WALKING: the supernatural ability to walk on hot coals without apparent pain or damage to the feet. Often firewalking is done in a hypnotic trance.

FORTUNE-TELLER: a seer; one who foretells events in an individual's life, usually for a fee.

GHOSTS: thought by many to be the spirits of the dead. In the light of biblical teaching, however, we may conclude that phenomena usually attributed to ghosts (furniture moving by itself, mystical lights, noises, and so on), are, if not in fact natural phenomena, really demonic manifestations.

GRAPHOLOGY: analysis of character through handwriting. Pure graphology is a scientific, rather than occult, practice. Occult graphologists, however, mix fortune-telling with handwriting analysis, and that is a demonic practice.

HEX: an evil spell; a curse.

HOROSCOPE: an astrological chart. Daily horoscopes are standard in most city newspapers. More involved, personalized charts may be purchased from professional astrologers (see Chapter 3).

HYPNOSIS: mental suggestion. The subject is put into a trancelike state, and the hypnotist is able to manipulate the subject's mind through speaking to his subconscious. Some trained medical personnel use hypnosis as therapy, and that is at best a questionable means of dealing with the human mind. But occult practitioners are able to use hypnosis for evil, supernatural purposes, and that is demonic.

MEDITATION: narrowing the focus of the mind in order to contemplate some truth or object. Meditation per se is not an occult activity; the Bible commands believers to meditate on the Word of God. But many occult practitioners also practice evil forms of meditation to gain greater demonic power.

MEDIUM: a person who acts as a channel of

communication between this world and the spirit world.

MYSTIC: a person involved with occult mysticism.

NECROMANCY: conjuring the spirits of the dead for communication. Necromancy was expressly forbidden in the Scriptures, and King Saul was condemned by God for practicing necromancy.

OBSERVER OF TIMES: the biblical term for an astrologer.

OCCULT: secret, mysterious, relating to supernatural forces.

OMENS: signs; supernaturally designed warnings of future events.

OUIJA BOARD: trademark name for a board used to obtain spiritualistic or telepathic messages. The players put their fingers on a special planchette that moves over a printed alphabet to spell out the messages.

PALMISTRY: *see* **Chiromancy.**

PARAPSYCHOLOGY: the study of occult phenomena and demonic manifestations.

POLTERGEIST: a mischievous "ghost" thought responsible for noises or movement of inanimate objects.

POTIONS: herb mixes, drugs, and concoctions with magical powers.

PSYCHIC PHENOMENA: events and powers that cannot be explained as normal physical occurrences and are attributed to spiritual powers.

REINCARNATION: the belief in rebirth of souls into new bodies after death.

RHABDOMANCY: divination by means of a wand or stick.

SABBAT: a meeting of witches to bring in new members.

SATANIC CHURCH: a church organized for the express purpose of worshiping the devil.

SATANISM: Satan worship. Usually satanic ritual is patterned after Christian rites. Satanists practice a form of baptism, and they have their own corrupt kind of communion service.

SEANCE: a meeting to practice necromancy; usually led by a medium.

SOOTHSAYING: foretelling events.

SORCERER: a wizard, witch, or magician; a practitioner of black magic.

SORCERY: use of demonic power to cast spells, perform black magic, conjure spirits, or practice other occult acts.

SPIRITUALISM: the belief that spirits of the dead can communicate with the living.

SUPERSTITION: an unwarranted belief in supernatural influence apart from God.

TALISMAN: a consecrated object, such as a ring or stone, bearing engraved figures or symbols supposed to bring good luck, keep away evil, and give supernatural powers. An amulet.

TAROT CARDS: special cards used in cartomancy.

TELEPATHY: communication by means of mind reading or other supernatural powers.

TRANSMIGRATION OF SOULS: reincarnation.

VOODOO: an ancient form of black magic practiced in primitive tribal areas.

WARLOCK: a male witch.

WHITE MAGIC: Magic ostensibly used for good purposes, such as healing, breaking spells, and so on (see Chapter 8). White magic is as unscriptural and demonic as black magic.

WITCH: one who practices magic, sorcery, and other black occult arts. Witches are often satanists.

WITCH DOCTOR: one who uses herbs, incantations, magic, voodoo, and sorceries to perform healing.

WIZARD: a sorcerer; a warlock.

YOGA: an oriental form of exercise and meditation that opens the mind to evil powers. The philosophy behind yoga is Buddhist, and many of the chants that go with it are atheistic and anti-Christian.

ZODIAC: the belt of planets and constellations that make up the astrological signs (see Chapter 3). The zodiac was based on a faulty and incomplete understanding of astronomy, but it remains unchanged in modern astrology.